Policy Forum Series – 37

AF764238

The 2000 Federal Budget:
Retrospect and Prospect

Editors
Paul A.R. Hobson and
Thomas A. Wilson

JOHN DEUTSCH INSTITUTE
FOR THE STUDY OF
ECONOMIC POLICY
QUEEN'S UNIVERSITY

INSTITUTE FOR
POLICY ANALYSIS
UNIVERSITY OF
TORONTO

ISBN: 0-88911-814-0 (bound) ISBN: 0-88911-816-7 (pbk.)

Queen's University, Kingston, Ontario K7L 3N6
Telephone: (613) 533-2294 FAX: (613) 533-6025
Printed and bound in Canada

Canadian Cataloguing in Publication Data

Main entry under title:

The 2000 federal budget : retrospect and prospect

(Policy forum series ; 37)
Proceedings of a conference held at Queen's University, Mar. 30-31, 2000.
Includes bibliographical references.
ISBN 0-88911-814-0 (bound) ISBN: 0-88911-816-7 (pbk.)

1. Budget - Canada - Congresses. I. Hobson, Paul A.R. (Paul Alexander Robert), 1953- . II. Wilson, Thomas A., 1935- . III. John Deutsch Institute for the Study of Economic Policy. IV. Series.

HJ2054.T86 2001 352.4'97103 C00-932339-2

Dedicated to the memory of
David Chadwick Smith

1931 - 2000

DAVID CHADWICK SMITH

On May 22, 2000, the economics profession, Queen's University and Canada lost David Chadwick Smith, one of its outstanding citizens, scholars and institution builders. Throughout his long career David Smith worked passionately and relentlessly, and typically out of the limelight, for the betterment of Canadian society.

The son of Baptist missionaries, David was born on August 12, 1931 in Ootacamund, India where the Smith family lived before returning to Simcoe, Ontario when David was eight years old. He attended public and high school in Simcoe and in 1953 graduated from McMaster University with an Honours Degree in Economics. It was while at McMaster that David met his wife, Mary Taylor. Armed with an MA from Oxford and a Ph.D. from Harvard, he taught briefly at Berkeley. David and Mary then came to Queen's in 1960. In 1968 he was named Head of Queen's Department of Economics, a position he held until 1981. In 1984, he was appointed Principal and Vice-Chancellor of Queen's. After leaving the Principalship in 1994, David also served as the Interim President and Vice-Chancellor of Trent University for 1997-98.

As Head of Economics, David transformed an already distinguished department into a major internationally recognized centre for economic research and teaching. The fact that a Queen's Ph.D. can be found on the masthead of virtually every Canadian university economics department is an integral part of David Smith's legacy to Canadian economics.

As Principal of Queen's from 1984 to 1994, David Smith enhanced the University's standing as one of the premier academic institutions in Canada. Among his many achievements were the Stauffer Library, the Biosciences

Complex, the National Scholars program, the International Study Centre at Herstmonceux, and the University's first women's studies program. As well, Dr. Smith was instrumental in the formation of the School of Policy Studies and, prior to becoming Principal, the John Deutsch Institute for the Study of Economic Policy.

David Smith was widely sought out as an advisor by both governments and universities over his more than 40-year career. He was a member of the Ontario Economic Council for ten years, including three as Deputy Chair, Vice-Chair of the Ontario Royal Commission on Workers' Compensation, and Director of Research (Economics) for the highly influential MacDonald Royal Commission. More recently, David was senior policy advisor to the Canada Millennium Scholarship Foundation and Chair of the advisory panel on postsecondary education in Ontario.

David Smith received many honours. In 1976, he was elected Fellow of the Royal Society of Canada, and, in 1994, was inducted as a Member of the Order of Canada. In recognition of his contributions to higher education and intellectual life generally, Dr. Smith was awarded honourary degrees by McMaster University, Queen's University at Belfast, the University of Western Ontario, Queen's University, and Loyalist College of Applied Arts and Technology.

In all of these myriad contributions, David always brought his patience, his expertise, his persuasive managerial talents and his wealth of insight to serve the greater good. But most of all, David Chadwick Smith will be remembered and loved as a kind and gentle and soft-spoken and generous soul. In dedicating this book to the memory of David Chadwick Smith, our thoughts and prayers also extend to Mary Smith, their two children, Monica and Geoffrey, and their three grandchildren on the loss of a beloved husband, father and grandfather.

In memory of David Smith, the Queen's Department of Economics plans to establish the David Chadwick Smith Chair in Economics. Any donations to this fund will be gratefully accepted by the Department of Economics.

ACKNOWLEDGEMENT

The 2000 Federal Budget: Retrospect and Prospect is ninth in the series of John Deutsch Institute (JDI) post-budget conferences and volumes. It is a pleasure to thank Thomas Wilson and Paul Hobson for coordinating and editing this volume. This is the third time that Tom has co-edited (and Toronto's Institute for Policy Analysis co-sponsored) a budget conference and volume. We were also fortunate that Paul Hobson, who was a Visiting Professor in the School of Policy Studies over the 1999-2000 academic year, also agreed to co-organize and co-edit the volume.

As always for JDI publications, everything revolves around Sharon Sullivan. She manages the conferences, coordinates the process of compiling the final versions of papers and then orchestrates the production of the final volume.

It is also a pleasure to thank Marilyn Banting for her editing skills and the School of Policy Studies' Publication Unit for valuable backup in preparing aspects of this volume.

On behalf of the JDI and Paul Hobson and Tom Wilson, I wish to acknowledge the marvellous cooperation we received from the contributors to the volume.

On a sad note, this volume is dedicated to the memory of David C. Smith who passed away on May 22, 2000. David played a pivotal role in founding the John Deutsch Memorial which eventually became the John Deutsch Institute for the Study of Economic Policy. Indeed, at the time of his death, David was serving as Acting Director of the JDI and in this capacity was overseeing this budget conference and this volume. David's contribution to the JDI was typical of the many varied ways he contributed so generously to the intellectual life of Canadian economics, Queen's University and the larger Canadian society.

Thomas J. Courchene
Director
John Deutsch Institute

TABLE OF CONTENTS

INTRODUCTION

Paul A.R. Hobson and Thomas A. Wilson

The John Deutsch Institute for the Study of Economic Policy (JDI) was fortunate to once again team up with the University of Toronto's Institute for Policy Analysis (IPA) in sponsoring this conference volume, *The 2000 Federal Budget: Retrospect and Prospect*.

The JDI has, since its inception, provided periodic assessments and evaluations of federal budgets. The 2000 federal budget was, of course, special as it marked the transition from the first to the second millennium. It was also special in that it was the first budget to deal with large potential future surpluses. Moreover, following previous budgets directed at planned deficit reduction and control, the focus at this forum, as in the recent public debate, shifted to the question of how to allocate the potential surplus.

The budget forum, held on March 30-31, 2000 at Queen's University, was a project in which David Smith took a personal interest during his term as Acting Director of the JDI. Typically, David was particularly interested in continuing the collaboration between JDI and IPA in hosting the forum and publishing its proceedings. He opened the forum and chaired its first session. His untimely death in May following the forum underscored for both of us the privilege of working with him to promote a tradition of strong policy analysis in Canada, surely part of his legacy to Canadian society.

It was a great pleasure to welcome Mrs. Stephanie Deutsch as an honorary participant at the conference. It was Harvey Lazar who noted that all the panellists in the first session had at some point worked at the Economic Council of Canada, once chaired by John Deutsch.

Session I: The 2000 Federal Budget: Implications for Canadian Federalism

The first session was a panel discussion, chaired by David Smith (Queen's). Panellists were Pierre Fortin (UQAM), Harvey Lazar (Queen's) and Tom Courchene (Queen's). Fortin focused his remarks on the interaction of fiscal and monetary policies under the inflation-targeting regime; his remarks are expanded in his presentation in Session VI. Lazar focused on the Social Union Framework Agreement (SUFA) between Ottawa and the provinces and its implications for the federal budgetary process. His argument was that there is a potential tension between the SUFA and the federal budgetary process — that the joint planning provisions of the SUFA will complicate the federal budget-making process, or that this process will undermine the joint planning provisions of the SUFA, or both. Courchene reviewed the provinces' reactions to federal tax cuts in light of provisions allowing the provinces to move to a tax on income (TONI) system rather than the tax-on-tax system.

Session II: The Budget and Its Macroeconomic Effects

The second session continued the tradition of JDI budget forums of looking at the macroeconomic effects of the budget. Chaired by Allan Gregory (Queen's), presentations were made by Thomas Wilson, Peter Dungan and Steve Murphy (IPA and University of Toronto) and Rick Egelton (Bank of Montreal). Gregor Smith (Queen's) served as commentator. Wilson, Dungan and Murphy underscored the point that much of what would traditionally have been included in the budget now occurs outside the budget process. They provided two sets of estimates, one for measures contained within the budget and one for what they term the "augmented budget", which combines measures contained within the budget itself with tax and spending initiatives implemented prior to the budget as well as prospective Employment Insurance (EI) payroll tax cuts over the next three years. They argued that the budget provides a very modest stimulus to real output under the inflation-targeting regime. They also argued that, over the medium term, the proposed tax changes are conducive to efficiency and economic growth. Egelton argued that while the federal budget provides some fiscal stimulus over the next two years, its impact on economic growth will be minimal in light of an anticipated tighter, offsetting monetary stance by the Bank of Canada. Smith explored the potential impacts of a decision to choose a faster pace of debt reduction, the changing composition of federal spending, and the role and quality of private sector forecasts (including those from IPA!) as a key element of the budgetary process.

Session III: The Taxation Dimension

The third session focused on the taxation dimension of the budget. Chaired by Ian Cromb (Queen's), presentations were made by Bill Robson (C.D. Howe Institute), Michael Smart (University of Toronto) and Robin Boadway (Queen's). Robson's presentation highlighted the time-release nature of the tax reductions announced in the budget. He argued that, in the course of the next couple of fiscal years, spending hikes dominate tax reductions, making lower marginal rates and greater fairness elusive policy goals. Smart explored the effect of tax reforms contained in the budget on the behaviour and welfare of families. He emphasized the importance of understanding the impact on economic efficiency through changes in effective marginal tax rates of measures such as changes to family benefits and the softening of foreign content restrictions for retirement savings. Boadway scrutinized the structural changes in the tax system contained in the budget against criteria for the design of a good tax system. He made a plea for increased emphasis on the use of refundable tax credits within the income tax system and for some consideration of the long-term implications of the ongoing shift of income tax room in favour of the provinces, especially in regard to the sustainability of the tax collection agreements.

Session IV: The Expenditure Dimension

The fourth session focused on the expenditure dimension of the budget. Chaired by France St-Hilaire (IRPP), presentations were made by Lars Osberg (Dalhousie) and Lise Bastarache (Royal Bank). Osberg picked up on what he perceives to be a discordance between the level and allocation of rhetorical and financial emphasis that runs through the budget. He argued that, if the budget is to lay out a plan for the new millennium, it must be both credible and sustainable, yet, in his view, there is a gulf between popular preferences (for the welfare state) and elite opinion (smaller government) which will continue to dog the budget-making process. Bastarache discussed the impact of supplements to the Canada Health and Social Transfer (CHST), including those contained in the 2000 federal budget, on the federal share in provincial revenues. She argued that federal cash transfer payments to the provinces through CHST and Equalization will continue to decline as a share of provincial revenues, notwithstanding the recent supplements. In that light, she argued that the provinces have done well to embrace TONI, since they will be forced to increasingly rely on own-source revenues for financing burgeoning social expenditures. Tom Courchene provided some remarks in the context of the information economy which are not reproduced in this volume, but see his book, *A State of Minds: Toward a Human Capital Future for Canadians* (Montreal: IRPP, 2001).

Session V: The Social Policy Dimension

An important aspect of the budget debate has been the future direction of social policy. Chaired by Kate Cuff (now at McMaster), presentations were made by Frances Woolley (Carleton), Michael Mendelson (Caledon Institute) and Keith Banting (Queen's). Woolley described the 2000 budget as a missed opportunity to deliver a coherent approach to family policy in Canada. She argued why a "children's budget" was wanted, needed, but not delivered. Mendelson's presentation is not reproduced in this volume, but see his Caledon Institute publication, *The Payback Budget of 2000*, co-authored with Ken Battle and Sherri Torjman. Banting took a broad perspective on the process of change in policy delivery over the past two decades — the reshaping of social Canada. He asked whether the myriad of incremental changes at the federal and provincial levels are adding up to a model of social policy that is internally coherent and politically sustainable and argued that we should not be sanguine if the answer is "no".

Session VI: Assessment and Perspectives

Assessments and perspectives were provided by Jim Stanford (CAW) and Pierre Fortin (UQAM), in the session ably chaired by Hugh Segal (IRPP). Fortin argued that fiscal stabilization policy is meaningless given flexible exchange rates and inflation targeting by the Bank of Canada. Rather, fiscal policy has implications for the composition of demand and output through its effect on the real rate of interest and the real exchange rate. Thus, the focus should be on the allocation of the fiscal dividend rather than on stabilization policy. In this regard, he argued, even more emphasis on debt reduction might have been appropriate. Stanford dubbed the 2000 budget the "tax cut" budget. He argued that the end result will be a lopsided society typical of the purely private economy and that the federal liberals have clearly indicated, through the 2000 budget, that this is how they *want* Canadian society to evolve.

Session VII: Budgeting in the New Millennium

Jack Mintz closed the forum with some remarks on the budget process and the fiscal issues confronting Canada in the new millennium. Appropriately, Mintz's remarks were completed following the October 2000 pre-election, mini-budget. While he gave high marks to the Martin budget process, he was critical of the lack of clarity and transparency (especially since the surplus is undefined), incremental decision-making, pro-cyclical rather than anti-cyclical fiscal policy, and a lack of clear fiscal objectives for planning. He called for an economic plan, complementary to the budget process. Elements of such a plan would include identifying the objects, debt reduction, a review of expenditure priorities, the need for tax reform rather than simply tax cutting, and some closure on federal-provincial fiscal relations.

Our Parting Remarks

As it turned out, the February 28, 2000 federal budget was followed by the mini-budget on October 18, 2000, which represented the Liberal economic platform in the subsequent general election. With the re-election of the Liberal government, the measures proposed in both budgets will be implemented as planned. Indeed, as of the time of writing, there is no plan for a 2001 federal budget.

We would like to express our sincere thanks to the authors and commentators for their cooperation in finalizing their papers. We would also like to thank the session chairs and participants from the floor for their contributions. It has always been the position of the JDI that it is the discussion from the floor that is central to the success of the Institute's conference activities. Marilyn Banting once again provided her editing skills in preparing this volume for publication and we thank her for a job well done. Finally, we wish to thank Sharon Sullivan for her superb work in keeping the project on track, taking care of all the administrative details, and in shepherding the authors and editors so as to bring about a most successful forum and the completion of this volume. Simply put, without Sharon there would have been no forum and no volume.

It is a pleasure for the JDI and IPA to have sponsored the forum and now to sponsor and publish this volume of retrospective and prospective assessments of the 2000 federal budget. We trust that it will contribute to the record of public policy development and analysis that was such an important thrust for both John Deutsch and David Smith.

Session One
THE 2000 FEDERAL BUDGET: IMPLICATIONS FOR CANADIAN FEDERALISM

THE SOCIAL UNION FRAMEWORK AGREEMENT AND THE FEDERAL BUDGETARY PROCESS

Harvey Lazar, Queen's University

This paper focuses on the impact and implications of the Social Union Framework Agreement (SUFA) for the federal budgetary process. The broad hypothesis here is that there is, or at least there is the potential for, a rather strong tension between the federal budget and SUFA, both in terms of process and content. And depending on the way in which this tension is dealt with, this could have important implications for the future of SUFA, for future federal budgets, or for both.

The paper is organized in three parts. The first part comments on the provisions of SUFA, including those that link it to the federal budgetary process. This part will explain why there is a potential tension between SUFA and federal budgets, especially on issues of *process*. Second, the 2000 federal budget is discussed to analyze the interaction between SUFA and that budget. Finally, the last part speculates on the implications of SUFA for the content of future federal budgets. Given that intergovernmental and direct transfers are a principal focus of SUFA and also typically the largest spending items in federal budgets, it is worth considering whether SUFA may have an impact on the extent to which these two different kinds of transfers are employed in future budgets.

SUFA and the Federal Budgetary Process

A few of SUFA's key features should be noted to help explain the linkage between SUFA and the federal budgetary process. To start with, SUFA is a political agreement between the federal government, nine provincial and two territorial governments. (Quebec chose not to sign the agreement and Nunavut had not yet signed when this chapter was being completed.) It does not, however, change the constitutional powers of any government. Nor is it legally binding.

As for the provisions of the agreement, most commentators would concur that SUFA is more about process — about how governments should relate to one another and to their citizens in the making of social policy — than it is about substantive new social policy commitments (see Marchildon, 2000). On the process side, SUFA calls for joint federal-provincial planning in social policy. It envisages a larger role for citizens and stakeholders in decision making and enhanced accountability and transparency. It also sets some new ground rules for the federal government's spending power and lays out general provisions for dispute avoidance and resolution. On the substantive side, it re-affirms the existing mobility provisions of the Agreement on Internal Trade and extends them significantly. More generally, it commits governments to certain principles, including the five principles associated with Canada's public health insurance system. To the extent that there is an overarching social policy principle, it may be related to the idea of equality of opportunity. This is not only reflected explicitly in section 1 of SUFA. It is also implicit in SUFA's mobility and spending power provisions (to be discussed below). In any event, if implemented effectively, SUFA offers the promise of better social policy (in the sense of more coherent and better-informed policy), more effective management of the federation and a better functioning democracy.

Two SUFA sections are particularly relevant for the purposes of this paper. One concerns the joint planning provisions referred to above and which are found in section 4 of the agreement. Among other things, these provisions call on signatory governments to:

Undertake joint planning to share information on social trends, problems and priorities and to work together to identify priorities for collaborative action.

Collaborate on implementation of joint priorities when this would result in more effective and efficient service to Canadians, including as appropriate joint development of objectives and principles, clarification of roles and responsibilities, and flexible implementation to respect diverse needs and circumstances, complement existing measures and avoid duplication. (SUFA, section 4)

In essence, these provisions anticipate social ministries at the federal, provincial and territorial levels working closely with one another. They also envisage governments consulting with one another before new social policies and programs are implemented if they are likely to affect other governments substantially.

The other relevant set of provisions concerns the decision rules around the use of the federal spending power for both intergovernmental and direct transfers.[1] These are found in section 5. They include a requirement that the Government of Canada consult with provincial and territorial governments at least one year prior to "renewal or significant funding changes in *existing* social transfers to provinces/territories ... and ... build due notice provisions into any new social transfers to provincial/territorial governments".[2] They also contain rules that govern *new* Canada-wide initiatives that Ottawa supports by transfers to the provinces. Among other things, these provisions call on governments to work collaboratively to identify Canada-wide priorities and objectives in health care, postsecondary education, social assistance and social services. They also state that new initiatives in these areas will need the agreement of at least six provinces. Finally, section 5 also requires the federal government to provide provinces and territories with at

---

[1]Since SUFA is a political agreement, not a legal one, a reviewer of this chapter challenged the use of the term "decision rules". The reviewer thought that the expression "principles of desirable behaviour" better captured the political commitments concerning the spending power.

[2]The quotation is from section 5 of SUFA. The emphasis on the word "existing" is mine.

least three months notice prior to implementing new direct transfers in these same areas and to consult. As the largest spending items in federal budgets often involve intergovernmental or direct transfers in the program areas noted above, there is now a significant connection between SUFA and the federal budget-making process.

The interaction between sections 4 and 5 of SUFA and federal budget-making entails, or has the potential to entail, tensions between the two orders of government because of the differences in their relative roles in these two processes, that is, the SUFA process and the federal budget process. In the case of SUFA, it is based on the idea that the two orders of government are partners in the federation and that there is "mutual respect between orders of government and a willingness to work more closely together to meet the needs of Canadians" (SUFA, preamble). Conversely, while the federal finance minister seeks a variety of inputs before he decides on and announces his budget, those consultations take place in a federally determined framework. It does not make sense to think that provinces can or should be full or equal partners in the overall making of a federal budget.

The SUFA recognizes this situation and attempts to deal with it in two ways. First, as already noted, section 4 provides for advance notice and consultation. Importantly, however, the undertakings for reciprocal notice and consultation are all subject to the qualification that they are to be made operational "in a manner consistent with the principles of our system of parliamentary government and the budget-making process". On the basis of this "carve-out" provision alone, the federal finance ministry appears to retain considerable freedom of action.[3]

At the same time, and this is the second point, section 5 imposes political limits on the freedom of the Government of Canada in its use of the spending power. In particular, in the case of new Canada-wide programs financed through intergovernmental transfers, the decision rule in section 5 appears to override the qualification or carve-out for the budgetary process referred

[3]There is no intention to suggest that the carve-out provision applies only to the federal government. It is understood that provincial and federal governments were interested in this "safety valve" and it applies to provinces as well as Ottawa. However, this chapter is focused on federal budget-making.

to in section 4 in the sense that advance notice and an offer to consult (both required by section 4) do not suffice. The agreement of a majority of provinces is also called for politically. An alternative way of making the same argument is to note that the section 4 commitments (covering any major change in social policy likely to affect another government substantially) apply to a broader range of potential initiatives than do those in section 5. But in relation to the narrower but still considerable range of initiatives financed through intergovernmental transfers, the section 5 provisions are more constraining on the federal government than is section 4, including in its budget-making. If this interpretation is correct, then the political constraints on the federal Finance ministry are somewhat stronger than the section 4 carve-out, read on its own, would suggest.

The above analysis is hypothetical. And we cannot forget that the constraints imbedded in SUFA are political, not legal. Governments have the power to ignore their political commitments if they judge, for whatever reason, that this is necessary. Therefore, a crucial issue that arises from the above is what kind of interaction is likely to emerge in practice between, on the one hand, the sections 4 and 5 provisions of SUFA and, on the other, the federal budget-making process. Here, one observation may be in order. For almost all of the 1990s, the federal Finance ministry was clearly in the driver's seat in terms of federal policy making in respect of social programs, including those financed through intergovernmental and direct transfers (Savoie, 1999; Greenspon and Wilson-Smith, 1996). The federal social departments were sometimes in the backseat and occasionally in the trunk. If future federal policy making does not entail a more even distribution of effective authority between the federal social and Finance ministries, it will be difficult for the federal social ministries to sustain the kind of joint planning discussions with their provincial counterparts that SUFA calls for. Provinces will have little reason to invest their political energy and incur the other transaction costs of joint planning if, in fact, the federal social ministries do not have the capacity to deliver on their commitments. Over the last year or two, there has been some evidence that, within the federal government, Health Canada and Human Resources Development Canada have been taking a lead role in defining the principles, objectives and accountability framework for the health care and early childhood development files. It remains to be seen, of course, whether this pattern is sustained.

The other provision of SUFA that affects the federal budget-making process directly has to do with "funding predictability". It provides that "the Government of Canada will consult with provincial and territorial governments at least one year prior to renewal or significant funding changes in existing social transfers to provinces/territories, unless otherwise agreed, and will build due notice provisions into any new social transfers to provincial/territorial governments" (SUFA, section 5). It is also noteworthy that the provisions of the SUFA that deal with dispute avoidance and resolution provide explicitly that those provisions cover matters related to "intergovernmental transfers". Considering that the political pressures that created SUFA originated with the announcement of large cuts in cash transfers to the provinces associated with the announcement of the Canada Health and Social Transfer (CHST) in the 1995 federal budget, it is noteworthy that the federal finance minister actually warned his provincial counterparts more than a year before his 1995 budget that substantial cuts would have to be made in intergovernmental transfers. Also, the actual cuts announced in the 1995 federal budget were not implemented until 1996. In other words, Paul Martin gave provinces more advance notice of transfer cuts than SUFA would have required had it then been in force. Where the CHST experience appears to fall well short of what SUFA requires is that the finance minister did not specify to the provinces in 1994 the magnitude of the cuts in transfers that he subsequently implemented. The heading "Funding Predictability" in section 5 of SUFA suggests that this kind of precision is called for in the future.

Summarizing on this first point, therefore, SUFA has been drafted to take into account the crosswalk between its own joint planning provisions and the federal budget-making process. In so doing, it strikes an interesting but ambiguous balance. On the one hand, it leaves significant leeway for the federal finance minister to continue with his budgetary process in much the way he did in pre-SUFA days, as it relates to new programs involving direct transfers. The requirement for advance notice is notice prior to implementation, not prior to the policy announcement, and this is not a high standard to meet. On the other, the advance notice provisions cut down considerably on the minister's freedom to spring another CHST-type surprise on the provinces, that is, a big reduction in intergovernmental transfers. And the decision rule on new Canada-wide programs financed through transfers from Ottawa to the provinces is also a new and potentially significant shift toward a more collaborative approach to social policy making. How this balance is interpreted and implemented by the federal government remains, of course, to be seen.

The 2000 Federal Budget

We shall consider now what the experience was in the 2000 federal budget. And we do so from the perspective of both what it said and what it did not say. First, the federal budget provided an additional $2.5 billion supplement to the CHST to help provinces and territories meet their commitments to health and higher education. The provincial governments had pressed the federal government for an increase in CHST in advance of the budget. In the event, the amount of the federal increase was much less than provincial governments would have liked. Moreover, they would have probably wanted the increase to be built into the base of the CHST (rather than being provided as a one-time supplement to be used over the next four years in any way that the provinces wanted for postsecondary education and health care). In any case, the CHST increase as such did not appear to be inconsistent with the federal government's obligations under SUFA.

The federal budget also anticipated $500 million more in equalization payments from Ottawa to the provinces. In the main, this reflected the simple working-out of the equalization formula rather than major changes in it. Once again, there was no inconsistency with SUFA.

Another major social policy announcement in the budget was the planned increase in the Canada Child Tax Benefit, which will see the maximum benefit for a family's first child grow from its current level of just over $1,800 to $2,400 in the year 2004. This was the product of an ongoing dialogue between federal and provincial governments and an outgrowth of the kind of joint planning that SUFA contemplates.

A further important announcement in the federal budget was the planned doubling in the duration of maternity and parental leave to one year under the Employment Insurance program. Federal expenditures under this program are based on the federal government's constitutional powers in relation to

Unemployment Insurance, not the federal spending power. This proposed measure was therefore presumably covered by the section 4 provisions on "Reciprocal Notice and Consultation" and not the section 5 provisions relating to the spending power. As already noted, the notice must be given and consultation must take place before the new or amended program's "implementation", not its announcement. This is not a heavy burden on the federal government and there is no indication that it was not met in this case. Indeed, the issue of maternity and parental benefits was part of the ongoing dialogue among federal, provincial and territorial governments associated with the children's agenda.[4]

What is perhaps equally interesting in the federal budget was its virtual silence on other aspects of the so-called Children's Agenda. On this item, the federal and provincial governments had been working together for some time to develop an action plan that would support early childhood development, expanded child care and other items. The fact that Martin did not announce additional policy initiatives in this area reflected what was then a temporary impasse between federal and provincial governments. Progress on issues related to early childhood development and other aspects of the Children's Agenda had at that time stalled.[5] In the absence of SUFA, it is not inconceivable that the federal government might have acted on its own in this area.

Thus, the 2000 federal budget contained fewer federal commitments to support provincial programming through the CHST than provinces would have liked. There clearly was a lot of tension between federal and provincial governments surrounding the future of health care in Canada and its financing. But SUFA was never expected to end political conflict on

---

[4]This does not mean that all provinces concurred in the proposed federal action, as subsequent statements by the Government of Quebec made clear.

[5]I have been provided with two overlapping but somewhat different interpretations for the lack of progress at the time of the 2000 federal budget. One interpretation is that provincial officials dealing with children's issues were being directed by their political masters from moving forward pending resolution of federal-provincial issues that were unrelated to children's policy. The second interpretation is that the federal-provincial planning process on the Children's Agenda had simply not been completed.

controversial issues. It establishes some guidelines for managing that conflict and for facilitating collaboration where that is possible. The 2000 federal budget was by no means a triumph for social policy in Canada. But it does appear to have respected the intergovernmental commitments, or at least the section 5 commitments relating to the spending power, made by the federal government in signing SUFA.

At the same time, to the extent that there were measures in the federal budget that reflected intergovernmental collaboration, as with the Canada Child Tax Credit, that collaboration began before the signing of SUFA and appears not to have been much influenced by SUFA. There were no other collaborative social policy initiatives in the budget that appear to have been influenced by the section 4 joint planning provisions of SUFA. In other words, it is not yet obvious that the more positive (joint planning) parts of SUFA affected the 2000 budget even though the budget did respect its spending power constraints.

The Future of the Federal Transfer System under SUFA

The final question to be discussed here is whether the SUFA provisions surrounding the spending power will change the shape of future federal budgets. At issue here is whether SUFA creates an incentive for Ottawa to prefer direct spending relative to intergovernmental transfers. The key point in this regard is that the section 5 provisions on intergovernmental transfers appear to constrain the federal government more than do that section's rules in respect of direct transfers to persons. Thus, one possible outcome is that future federal budgets will lean more to direct transfers and less to intergovernmental transfers than they have in the past. Such an outcome would be attractive to those who call for a strong federal government and who want to strengthen the direct relationship between Ottawa and the citizenry.

While this incentive appears real, it can also be exaggerated. In discussions with officials from both orders of government who were involved in the SUFA negotiations, they emphasized that the provisions of section 5 should not be read on their own but in connection with the spirit and letter of the whole agreement.[6] The spirit is captured in the preamble (cited earlier) that refers to the agreement as one "based upon a mutual respect between orders of government and a willingness to work more closely together to meet the needs of Canadians". And the letter includes the section on "Joint Planning and Collaboration" quoted above. So the apparently less constraining rules on *direct* transfers may not be much different in practice than the limits on new "Canada-wide initiatives supported by transfers to provinces". Furthermore, it also bears noting that if the counterfactual to SUFA is the *status quo ante*, then the new rules that require the federal government to give three months' advance notice and consult on direct transfers are more constraining on Ottawa than was the situation prior to SUFA. This is simply because there were no rules previously, just federal practices that varied from situation to situation and program to program.

A further consideration is that SUFA requires that programs financed through intergovernmental transfers be subject to the same kind of accountability mechanism that applies to direct transfers. Historically, it had been easier to get clear accountability relationships with direct transfers, since only one order of government was involved. In fact, within Ottawa prior to SUFA, the absence of accountability provisions for programs financed through transfers to other orders of government had begun to create an incentive for the federal government to prefer direct transfers. In this particular respect (accountability provisions), SUFA may have weakened an incentive structure favouring direct transfers over intergovernmental transfers.

In any case, under the new rules, Ottawa would have been compelled to give notice of the Millennium Scholarship Fund and to afford provinces the opportunity to identify potential duplication and to propose alternative approaches to implementation. How different this would have been as compared to the way in which the Millennium Fund has in fact been introduced is unclear, however, as in the actual case the federal government was also open to negotiation about the modalities of the implementation. In any event, formal notice and consultation provisions under the terms of the

---

[6]This is based on the author's interviews with provincial and federal negotiators.

framework agreement more or less assure provinces that a new federal proposal will attract public attention if the provinces want the proposal to get that attention. And if provincial views are dismissed out of hand, Ottawa will be seen to be making light of SUFA. At the same time, it is equally the case that "advance consultation" rules do not guarantee provinces a particular outcome.

In the short run, perhaps for the life of the Liberal government now in office in Ottawa, direct spending may be preferred to new intergovernmental transfers. To the extent that this is true, the political reasons would presumably include the government's belief that some strengthening of its direct link to individual citizens is important. Recent evidence includes the Millennium Scholarship Fund, the federal government's increasing transfers for the National Child Benefit and its proposal to enrich Employment Insurance (EI) benefits for maternity and parental leave.[7] The federal government may also attach some weight to the idea that political accountability for spending is greater when the government that taxes spends directly rather than acting through another level of government. But once again, even under Jean Chrétien's government, this tendency can be exaggerated.[8] The Equalization program was one of the very few in Ottawa that was not cut during the first mandate of the federal Liberals. Ottawa poured substantial money back into CHST in the 1999 and 2000 budgets. When this chapter was being completed (in the summer of 2000), federal spokesmen were promising further substantial CHST contributions for health. So recent experience suggests that the federal government is by no means relying exclusively on the direct transfer approach.

Provincial governments may also lean the other way. They will not want new heavily conditioned transfers from the federal government. But SUFA does

---

[7]These are quite different from one another. The Millennium Scholarship Fund was an example of unilateral federal action and the Canada Child Benefit is an example of federal-provincial collaboration, both based on the federal spending power. The EI initiative is based on a federal head of power under section 92 of the *Constitution Act, 1982*.

[8]Offsetting this point is the above argument that SUFA creates enhanced requirements for political accountability for programs financed through inter-governmental transfers.

not contemplate heavily conditioned transfers. Rather, it anticipates both orders of government agreeing on Canada-wide objectives, the federal government committing to and transferring funds to the provinces to assist them in pursuing those objectives, provinces then designing and delivering their own programs to achieve the objectives and public accountability for the results. So the new transfers will not be unconditional. But the conditions are expected to be general (more like the *Canada Health Act* conditions than the tighter cost-sharing rules under the Canada Assistance Plan). And provinces will have played a larger role in shaping them than was the case with earlier programs. In many situations, provinces will prefer this kind of intergovernmental transfer to a direct transfer.

Given the apparent leanings of both orders of government, a plausible outcome is that both direct and intergovernmental transfers will be with us for a long time. And the choice of instrument will depend not only on the kinds of broad arguments set out above but also on the specifics of the individual files in question.

In fact, the data for the last few years do not suggest that there has been a marked trend one way or the other. When the Liberals came to power in 1993, cash transfers to other governments were 24% of federal program spending. They then rose to 25% in 1995, probably because federal government cuts in its own programs were implemented faster than its cuts in transfers to the provinces. They subsequently dropped to 20% in 1998 as a result of the transfer reductions but have since risen to 23%. For direct transfers to persons, the 1993 number is 42% and it has since risen to 43%. Given the aging of the population, and the importance of direct transfers to senior citizens as a percentage of all direct transfers by Ottawa, this increase suggests no overall bias toward direct over intergovernmental transfers.

Conclusions

In summary, there is a tension between the federal budgetary process and SUFA. There are reasons to worry that either the joint planning provisions of SUFA will complicate the federal budget-making process or, more likely, that the federal budget-making process will undermine that section of SUFA. A glance at the 2000 federal budget suggests, however, that this tension was well managed in the preparations for that document. Also, a quick analysis of trends in federal spending on direct and intergovernmental transfers suggests that, to date, the mix of these two kinds of transfers has not changed significantly as a result of SUFA.

To date, there has been no independent analysis of the influence of SUFA's joint planning provisions on the conduct of federal-provincial relations. Based on conversations with federal and provincial officials, it appears that the joint planning provisions are not yet having an important impact. There is a lot of federal-provincial social policy work underway, but it is not clear that SUFA is having a large effect on that work. Assuming that this comment on the joint planning provisions has a measure of truth about it, this would argue that the compatibility of the SUFA joint planning provisions and the federal budget-making processes has not yet been tested fully. Moreover, unless the joint planning provisions become more robust, there will be no basis for determining the compatibility of the two processes.

The next federal budget will be prepared against a backdrop of a large federal budgetary surplus. If that budget can be prepared in a manner consistent with the federal government's SUFA undertakings relating to the spending power, this will be a reasonably good indicator that federal budget-making and Ottawa's SUFA spending power commitments can comfortably co-exist.

References

A Framework to Improve the Social Union for Canadians (SUFA), An agreement between the Government of Canada and the Governments of the Provinces and Territories, February 4, 1999.

Greenspon, E. and A. Wilson-Smith (1996), *Double Vision: The Inside Story of the Liberals in Power* (Toronto: Doubleday Canada).

Marchildon, G. (2000), "Reply to Ryan and Burelle: A Step in the Right Direction", *Inroads: A Journal of Opinion* 9.

Savoie, D. (1999), *Governing From the Centre: The Concentration of Power in Canadian Politics* (Toronto: University of Toronto Press).

TAXATION, FISCAL FEDERALISM AND THE 2000 FEDERAL AND PROVINCIAL BUDGETS

Thomas J. Courchene, Queen's University and Institute for Research on Public Policy

Introduction

My assigned role is to address and assess the fiscal federalism issues arising from the 2000 budget cycle. Towards this end, the first part of my comments will highlight selected aspects of Paul Martin's February 28, 2000 federal budget. I will then attempt to detail the manner in which the various provinces have responded in their respective budgets. Emphasis will largely be on the provinces' new rate and bracket structures as part of the shift from "tax on tax" to "tax on base". Finally, I shall offer some reflections on these developments as they relate to a series of issues associated with Canadian fiscal federalism.

The 2000 Federal Budget

The 2000 federal budget was an important fiscal bellwether, in part because it marked the break between the successful series of post-1995 budgets designed to tame the deficit and the presumed set of future budgets that must deal with how to spend the surplus. In part, also, the 2000 budget was significant since it had as one of its principal goals the reform of the income tax system, both personal and corporate.

Prior to focus on the budget's substance, a few words related to process are in order. The formal or parliamentary part of the federal budget cycle began with Paul Martin's November 2, 1999 *Economic and Fiscal Update* presented before the House of Commons Finance Committee in London, Ontario. What made this *Update* significant is that Martin departed from his traditional two-year horizon and presented estimates of the likely budget surpluses over a five-year horizon. (As an aside, while the cumulative value of these projected surpluses was truly impressive at the time — roughly $70 billion in the context of provisions for prudency and the Contingency Reserve and in excess of $100 billion in terms of the "raw" estimates — they pale in terms of more recent estimates of the surplus.) In terms of the priorities of the portion of this surplus allocated to tax reduction, Martin's focus was on personal (PIT) rather than corporate income taxation and, within the PIT system, on generating tax relief for low- and middle-income taxpayers.

The next step in the parliamentary process was the release in December 1999 of *Budget 2000: New Era ... New Plan*, the report of the House of Commons Finance Committee chaired by Maurice Bevilacqua. This report significantly moved the taxation yardsticks by emphasizing the need for corporate tax cuts, for capital gains tax cuts and for reducing high income surcharges. Because there is an obvious link between the Liberal majority on the Finance Committee and the minister of finance, the committee plays an important role in the budget process. For example, it can "street test" new proposals and its recommendations can also reflect the evolution of Finance's thinking on budget measures so that there are few surprises, or at least few "negative" shocks on budget day. However, the Finance Committee's role in the 2000 budget process was especially important because of the rapidly changing nature of the Canadian economy. In particular, there were growing concerns about our faltering productivity (relative to the United States), as well as the "brain drain". In my view, it was this rapidly changing environment that drove the committee's recommendations and, later, the budget itself in the direction of being concerned more about lowering marginal rates on mobile factors. As I will argue below, the budget still fell well short on this score.

Nonetheless, the February 28, 2000 federal budget did contain one "positive shock" or surprise, namely the indexation of the personal income tax system for inflation. Perhaps it should not have come as a surprise, since Stockwell Day's earlier Alberta budget (February 24, 2000) also embodied indexation.[1] Moreover, the November 1999, *Final Report and Recommendations* of the Saskatchewan Personal Income Tax Review Committee also recommended that Saskatchewan's new "tax on income" be fully indexed, which it duly was in the province's March 29, 2000 budget. In any event, Martin's 2000 budget not only indexed the PIT system for inflation but did so in a manner that ensured that the basic personal deductions as well as the thresholds for the middle- and high-income tax brackets were increased to values that (roughly) would have prevailed had the system not been de-indexed from 1988 onward.

Details with respect to indexation as well as the other key tax measures contained in the 2000 budget appear in Tables 1 and 2. Table 1 presents the five-year tax-reduction plan while Table 2 provides details on those aspects of the five-year plan that were part of the two-year legislative program pursuant to the budget. Apart from indexation, the major provisions are as follows (the five-year framework provision is listed first, followed in parentheses by the legislative or Table 2 provisions):

- a reduction in the middle-income tax rate from 26% to 23% (from 26% to 24% on July 1, 2000);

- an increase in the Canada Child Tax Benefit from $1,805 to $2,400 (to $2,056 on July 1, 2000 and then to $2,265 on July 1, 2001);

- eliminate the 5% federal surtax (eliminate the 5% surtax on incomes up to $85,000 on July 1, 2000 and reduce the rate to 4% on incomes above this level on January 1, 2001);

- reduce the corporate tax rate from 28% to 21% (reduce corporate tax rate from 28% to 27% on January 1, 2001);

---

[1]Although the indexing of a single-rate tax involves only the indexation of personal, spousal and other deductions.

Table 1: Five-Year Tax-Reduction Plan

Areas for Action	*Actions Proposed To Be Implemented over the Next Five Years*	*Amount of Annual Tax Relief in 2004-05 (millions of dollars)*
Eliminate automatic increases in the tax burden due to inflation	• Immediately restore full indexation of the tax system effective January 1, 2000 • Increase the amount of income Canadians can earn tax-free to at least $8,000 for the basic personal amount and at least $6,800 for the spousal/equivalent-to-spouse amount	See below 2,760*
Reduce the high tax burden at the middle-income level	• Reduce to 23% the 26%-middle tax rate • Increase the level of income at which the middle tax rate begins to apply from $29,590 to at least $35,000 • Increase the level of income at which the top tax rate begins to apply from $59,180 to at least $70,000 • Eliminate the 5% surtax	3,600 2,940* 730* 865
Increase support for children	• Increase support for children under the Canada Child Tax Benefit over the course of the next five years, with maximum benefits rising to $2,400 for the first child	2,525*
Make the Canadian economy more internationally competitive	• Reduce the corporate income tax rate by seven percentage points to 21% from 28% on business income not currently eligible for special tax treatment • Reduce the capital gains inclusion rate from three-quarters to two-thirds • Postpone taxation of gains on shares acquired under qualifying stock options to when shares are sold rather than when options are exercised • Allow tax-free rollover of capital gains on qualified investments from one small business to another	2,995 295 75 75
Other	• Technical measures including other indexation	780*
Total Of which indexation contributes		17,640 6,215

Note: *Amounts include indexation, based on assumed annual inflation rate of 1.8%.
Source: Martin (2000, Table 4.1).

Table 2: Summary of Budget 2000 Tax Measures

Areas for Action	*Actions Proposed To Be Legislated through the 2000 Budget*	*Amount Annually in 2004 (millions)*
Eliminate automatic increases in the tax burden due to inflation	• Restore full indexation to the tax system effective January 1, 2000 • Indexation is expected to result in increases to the amount of income Canadians can earn tax-free to about $8,000 for the basic personal amount and $6,800 for the spousal/equivalent-to-spouse amount	See below 2,015*
Reduce the high tax burden at the middle-income level	• Reduce to 24% the 26% tax rate effective July 1, 2000 • Increase the level of income at which the middle tax rate begins to apply from $29,500 to $32,000 • Increase the level of income at which the top tax rate begins to apply from $59,180 to $64,000 • Eliminate the 5% deficit reduction surtax for incomes up to about $85,000 effective July 1, 2000, and reduce the 5% surtax rate to 4% on the tax payable on incomes above that level effective January 1, 2001	2,410 1,885* 300* 365
Increase support for children	• Increase the maximum Canada Child Tax Benefit: – to $2,056 by July 1, 2000 from $1,805 – to $2,265 by July 1, 2001 • Increase benefits to middle-income taxpayers through: – increases to the base benefit and – increases to the level of income at which benefits begin to be reduced	2,175*
Make the Canadian economy more internationally competitive	• Reduce the corporate income tax rate to 27% from 28% on business income not currently eligible for special tax treatment effective January 1, 2001 • Reduce the corporate income tax rate to 21% effective January 1, 2001 on active business income between $200,000 and $300,000 earned by a small business • Reduce the capital gains inclusion rate from three-quarters to two-thirds • Postpone taxation of gains on shares acquired under qualifying stock options to when shares are sold rather than when options are exercised • Allow tax-free rollover of capital gains on qualified investments from one small business to another	455 100 295 75 75
Other	• Technical measures including other indexation	780*
Total Of which indexation contributes		**10,930** **6,215**

Note: *Amounts include indexation, based on an assumed annual inflation rate of 1.8%.
Source: Martin (2000, Table 4.2).

- reduce capital gains inclusion rate from 75% to 66.75% (implemented immediately, i.e., July 1, 2000);

- postpone taxation of gains on shares acquired under qualifying stock options to when shares are sold rather than when options are exercised (implemented immediately).

All in all, a very significant tax reduction exercise, with the cost of those measures implemented in the budget accounting for roughly two-thirds of the projected costs of the full five-year program (e.g., $10.9 billion vs. $17,640 billion in 2004, from the last column of the tables).

The combination of restoring full indexation and the middle-income tax cut, among other provisions, ensured that the budget would be well received by Canadians. Indeed, it attracted only one query in Question Period before the opposition parties refocused their attention on the then-ongoing Human Resources Development Canada (HRDC) scandal.[2]

If the budget attracted little criticism from the other federal parties, in contrast it had very important implications for the provincial budgets. One of these related to the ongoing transition from the old tax-on-tax approach to the shared federal-provincial PIT system to the new tax-on-income approach. When fully in place, one feature of the rate-and-bracket freedom under tax on income is that federal changes in tax rates and tax brackets will not affect provincial taxation. However, as is clear from Table 2, several of the key federal tax changes that took effect on July 1, 2000 will, other things remaining unchanged, impact on the provincial tax systems. For example, the reduction in the middle-income tax rate from 26% to 24% as well as much of the indexation took effect on July 1, 2000. Absent specific provincial initiatives, these federal tax measures will imply provincial tax cuts. Hence, an important part of the following section relating to provincial budgets will focus on the variety of ways in which the provinces addressed this spillover.

---

[2]One area that did eventually generate considerable opposition was the once-and-for-all approach to health-care funding. However, this opposition was situated more in the federal-provincial arena than in the House of Commons.

A second link between the federal and provincial budgets is admittedly more speculative and it relates to my earlier assessment (Courchene, 2000) of the 2000 federal budget as a "Paul Martin Sr. budget". Underlying this label is my view that as important as indexation and reducing taxes on low- and middle-income Canadians are, these measures are more attuned to the needs of Canada in the Paul Martin Sr. era. Taxation in the millennium must go beyond this and embrace the notion that stemming the brain drain and the jobs drain requires that our taxes on mobile factors become more competitive. To an important degree, some of the requisite provisions on the competitive front are in the five-year plan. Hence, the real concern then becomes one of why so little of the Table 1 five-year plan as it relates to mobile factors (corporations and high-level human capital) is incorporated into the legislative program in Table 2. As one perceptive commentator noted, back-loading both the corporate tax cuts and the phase-out of the high-income surcharge places these initiatives on "government time", while the world is now ticking on "Internet time".

Perhaps this assessment is too harsh. After all, the budget went much further in terms of addressing tax competitiveness than did Martin's November *Economics and Fiscal Update*. Indeed, the provision that places the taxation of stock options on the same footing as that in the United States was not even part of the Finance Committee's recommendations — it came into being as a result of a plea from Nortel's John Roth to ensure that Canada becomes a more favourable environment for employing our human capital. This aside, the timid decrease in corporate tax rates from 28% to 27% on January 1, 2001, will leave Canada well above all of its G7 partners in terms of tax rates in the fast-growing services sector. This is surprising since corporate tax cuts are not very expensive in terms of forgone tax dollars (and if Ireland is an example, tax cuts could even *increase* corporate tax revenues). Moreover, since we all know that Canada eventually has to get its corporate rates down to competitive levels, this argues strongly for a first-mover advantage. But this would have been clearly off-side with the overall low-and-middle-income approach that drove the 2000 budget. Beyond this, the failure to remove the high-income surtax immediately, let alone decrease the top marginal rate, underscores the social policy, as distinct from a wealth-creation perspective underpinning the budget.

What this effectively does, therefore, is transfer responsibility for wealth creation to those provinces whose economic futures are in jeopardy unless these top marginal rates come down.

I now turn to the various provincial budgets where the focus will be on the manner in which they responded to the tax-on-income issue and to the competitiveness challenges articulated in the previous paragraphs.

The 2000 Provincial Budgets

The obvious starting point for a quick *tour d'horizon* of provincial budgets is Alberta. One reason for this is that this was the first of the provincial budgets — February 24, 2000, even before the February 28, federal budget. A more important reason is that Alberta had spent more time than most provinces in terms of thinking about the transition to a tax on income, including the 1998 report of the *Alberta Tax Review Committee* whose findings led to the single-rate tax in Stockwell Day's 2000 Alberta budget. I shall then focus on the other provinces (in no particular order) and with varying degrees of detail. While the responses in the provinces' 2000 budgets probably set the general pattern for how their tax-on-income systems will evolve, many of these budgets are nonetheless in the nature of immediate-term responses. Phrased differently, a year or so out, there will be an important analytical and empirical paper to be written about the new tax-on-income equilibrium.

Alberta

The Alberta tax-on-income regime is simple and straightforward, albeit controversial politically and problematic in terms of its implications for other provinces. Essentially, the 2000 Alberta budget proposed that, for calendar year 2001:

- Alberta will have an 11% single-rate tax system. Since the budget, this has been lowered to a 10.5% single-rate or flat tax. The reason for this is that one of the underlying PIT reform principles was that *all* Alberta taxpayers were to be better off under the single-rate tax than they would be if the tax-on-tax system were continued. Because the federal budget (which followed the Alberta budget) reduced middle-income-bracket tax rates, some middle-income Albertans would have been better off in terms of the status quo. Hence the post-budget reduction in the flat tax from 11% to 10.5%.

- Despite the single-tax, the new regime will remove close to 200,000 Albertans from the tax rolls. This is because the basic personal and spousal credits have been substantially increased. The basic personal credit will rise from $7,131 to $11,620 and the spousal credit will also be set at $11,620. Moreover, the tax rates for implementing these credits is, of course, the 10.5% rate. This is a much higher rate for implementing the credit than under the former tax-on-tax regime. This combination of a flat or single-rate tax and identical personal and spousal exceptions implies that family income will essentially be taxed (for Alberta's share of the PIT) the same regardless of whether this income is earned by one or both spouses. This "neutrality" has long been a goal of Alberta tax reform.

- All surcharges as well as the existing "flat tax" are removed.

- The personal and spousal exemptions are indexed to the consumer price index (CPI).

The result of the Alberta budget is that the top combined marginal tax rate in Alberta will now be 39.5%: 29% federal and 10.5% provincial (ignoring any remaining federal surcharges).

One final comment is in order. Despite the quite dramatic approach that Alberta has taken to restructuring its PIT, there was no sentiment at all on the part of Albertans (as reflected in the hearings associated with the Alberta Tax Review Committee) for the province to pull out of the Tax Collection Agreements and to mount its own, separate, PIT system.

The first province to react to Alberta was one that, arguably, is among the most affected by Alberta's flat tax, namely Saskatchewan.

Saskatchewan

Like Alberta, Saskatchewan also struck a committee to review its personal income tax in the context of the new tax-on-income system — the Personal Income Tax Review Committee, chaired by Jack Vicq — which reported in November of 1999. The challenge facing the Vicq Committee was not only to design a tax-on-income approach to the PIT that reflected the priorities and needs of Saskatchewan residents but, as well, to design a system that was not too far offside with the new PIT reality in Alberta. The March 29, 2000 Saskatchewan budget (which adopted the basic recommendations of the Vicq Committee) contained the following provisions:

- Simpler, lower provincial tax rates applied to taxable income will replace the current system's Basic Saskatchewan Tax, Flat Tax, Debt Reduction Surtax, High Income Surtax and low-income reduction.

- Tax Rates:
  11% - on taxable income of $35,000 or less
  13% - on taxable income between $35,000 and $100,000
  15% - on taxable income over $100,000.

- Higher personal tax credit amounts will focus support on the family, including:
  - a basic personal tax credit of $8,000;
  - a spousal (or equivalent) tax credit of $8,000;
  - a new $2,500 per child tax credit; and,
  - a $1,000 seniors supplement to the age credit.

- An 11% tax rate will be applied to taxable capital gains on qualified farm property and small business shares exceeding the lifetime $500,000 capital gains deduction.

- Inflation protection will be introduced once the tax system is fully implemented through the indexation of the provincial income brackets and personal tax credits.

Among the significant implications of this tax reform are that Saskatchewan's top marginal rate falls from 19.9% to 15%. While this is admittedly much higher than the 10.5% Alberta tax rate, the fact that the top marginal rate kicks in only at $100,000 provides some further offset. These tax reforms will be phased in over three years.

Of special interest is the provision that the tax rate applicable to capital gains on the sale of farms and small businesses will be 11%, irrespective of the income level of the seller. It seems to me that this is an attempt by Saskatchewan to define "income" for tax purposes, an initiative that would not have been allowed under the old tax-on-tax regime and also runs counter to the spirit of the federal government's interpretation of tax on income. This issue will be explored further, in the context of Ontario's proposals for redefining income for tax purposes.

Note finally that, as was the case for Alberta, Saskatchewan will allow the 2000 federal tax cuts to "pass through" to the provincial tax system, that is, for all intents and purposes Saskatchewan remains on a tax-on-tax system for the calendar year 2000.

British Columbia

British Columbia had already committed itself to reduce the single tax rate under the tax-on-tax system to 49.9%. Under the new federal tax rates for 2000 (i.e., 17, 25, 29),[3] British Columbia's altered tax rates become 8.4%, 12.4% and 14.4%, where these three rates are 49.9% of the above federal rates. In addition, for year 2000 British Columbia will retain its two surtaxes — 30% of tax in excess of $5,300 and an additional 15% of tax in excess of $8,600. For calendar year 2001, British Columbia will shift to a "full" tax-on-income approach, that is, it will convert the surtaxes into the rate and bracket structure, which will generate an additional two tax brackets. Thus, British Columbia's rate and bracket structure for 2001 will be as follows: 8.4% for taxable income up to $30,335; 11.9% between $30,335 and $60,670; 16.7% between $60,670 and $70,000; 18.7% between $70,000 and $85,000; and 19.7% for taxable income over $85,000. This rate and bracket

---

[3]While the middle-income federal tax rate fell from 26% to 24% on July 1, the "average" middle-income tax rate for 2000 is 25%.

structure will be fully indexed (and the above bracket thresholds assume an inflation rate of 1.1% over the current year).

On the corporate tax side, the small business tax rate will be reduced to 4.75% (from 5.5%), which made British Columbia's small business tax rate the lowest in Canada. However, one must add "to this point in time" to this claim since, over the provincial budget cycle, several provinces with later budgets also made this same claim as they lowered their small business tax rate (e.g., to 4.5% in New Brunswick).

Manitoba

For calendar year 2000, Manitoba will adopt three tax rates — 8%, 12.22% and 13.63% — and will retain its existing 2% net income tax (often referred to as a "flat" tax) and the 2% surtax on net income over $30,010. In 2001, the system will incorporate the 2% net income tax and the 2% surtax in a three-bracket rate structure: 10.9% on taxable income up to $30,544; 16.2% between $30,544 and $61,089; and 17.5% for taxable incomes over $61,089. Manitoba is also committed to reduce the middle-income tax rate to 15.6% for calendar year 2002. In addition, Manitoba not only indexes the new system for inflation, but increases its non-refundable tax credits by nearly 40%, effectively offsetting many years of "bracket creep".

New Brunswick

Prior to the federal budget, New Brunswick had a 60% PIT rate under the tax-on-tax regime. Expressed in terms of a tax-on-income approach, this 60% rate would convert to the following three tax rates: 10.2%, 15.6% and 17.4%. However, part of the election platform that brought Premier Lord to power committed his government to reducing the rate from 60% to 57%. With this commitment already in place, the New Brunswick budget did not allow the federal budget cuts to directly influence provincial taxes. Rather, as I understand the New Brunswick budget, the 57% tax rate will be applied to the pre-existing federal tax rates (i.e., to 17, 26 and 29, not to 17, 24 and 29) and tax brackets. This yields a tax-on-income rate structure of 9.68%, 14.82%, 17.4%, which will apply in 2001. For year 2000, New Brunswick will split the difference between the 60% and 57% rates, that is, 9.94%, 15.21% and 16.96%. There is also an 8% high-income surtax.

The budget makes clear that this is only an interim approach. It appears that the province will begin a consultative approach with an eye to designing its tax-on-income structure (e.g., number of brackets, income thresholds, degree of progressivity, etc.). One of the issues to be addressed by this consultative process will be the future of the 8% surtax, one option of which is to convert it into a fourth tax bracket.

Prince Edward Island

As a result of commitments made in 1999, PEI lowered its PIT tax rate from 58.5% to 57.5% (effective January 1, 2000). Since the province's tax system remains on a tax-on-tax basis for 2000, this means that PEI taxpayers will benefit from their own tax-rate reduction as well as the reduction in provincial taxes arising from the federal budget changes. In year 2001, PEI will formally shift over to a tax on income by applying the 57.5% tax rates to the federal tax rates to create three tax rates for PEI: 9.8%, 13.8% and 16.7% (i.e., 57.5% of 17, 24 and 29). At least for an interim period, PEI will also retain its existing surtax as part of the tax-on-income system.

Nova Scotia

From a Nova Scotia budget bulletin *Tax on Income* (April 11, 2000):

> Starting in the 2000 taxation year, Nova Scotia will move to a tax on income (TONI) system of assessing personal income tax. The new system will apply a Nova Scotia tax to the federally determined taxable income. The previous system applied provincial tax as a percentage of federal tax.
>
> Nova Scotia will set tax on income rates for the 2000 tax year to be equivalent to the effective tax-on-tax rates in place in 1999. Nova Scotia will also use the 1999 brackets to determine when the rates apply.

The Nova Scotia tax rate for 1999 was 57.5% (reduced from a peak of 59.5%). Thus, its tax rates for 2000 will be 9.8%, 14.95%, 16.7%. Note that the middle-income tax rates is 57.5% of the former federal rate of 26%, not the 2000 budget rate of 24%. Moreover, as the above quotation indicates, Nova Scotia will *not* buy into the federal indexing of bracket thresholds. In other words, Nova Scotia has effectively prevented the federal tax reductions from being passed through to provincial taxes. Presumably, the government's priorities run in terms of achieving budget balance, so that from this perspective it could not afford to "pass through" the federal reductions to its own part of the PIT. Beyond this, the existing 10% surtax for high-income taxpayers will remain in place.

Newfoundland

In the fall of 1999,[4] the Government of Newfoundland and Labrador published its mid-fiscal-year financial statement which included the following provisions relating to PIT reform:

> The government intends to reduce the basic personal income tax rate from 69 percent of basic federal tax to 49 percent, plus surtaxes over the next three years. As of January 1, 2000, the basic personal rate of tax will be reduced from 69 percent of the basic federal tax to 62 percent. On January 1, 2001, the province will likely move to a Tax on Income system. However, the basic rate will be the equivalent of 55 percent of the Basic Federal Tax. In 2002, the rate will be the equivalent of 49 percent of the Basic Federal Tax. We will, over three years, move our basic rate of tax from 69 percent to 49 percent of the federal tax. To provide for greater equity among taxpayers at the lower income levels and to make this change affordable, we will implement gradually increasing surtaxes each year.

As I interpret this, the tax-on-income equivalent tax rates for Newfoundland in year 2000 will be 10.54%, 15.5% and 17.98% plus surtaxes. The 2001 tax rates will be 9.35%, 13.2% and 15.95% and the equivalent of 49% of basic federal tax for 2002 implies rates of 8.33%, 11.76% and 14.21% with, as the above quotation notes, "increasing surtaxes".

---

[4]Perhaps there has been an update on Newfoundland tax-on-income proposals to take account of the 2000 federal budget, but I could not find one.

Ontario

Table 3 presents the recent history of Ontario personal income tax cuts. As of January 1, 2000 (i.e., pre-budget), the tax-on-income equivalent rates were 6.545%, 10.01% and 11.165%. Ontario responded to the 2000 federal budget by moving to a tax-on-income approach for 2000. Among the features of Ontario's new tax system are:

- Establishing bracket thresholds for year 2000 of $30,004 and $60,009 for the second and third bracket respectively. These will be indexed. Note that these bracket widths differ from the federal brackets (see Table 2).

- Enacting a 5% cut on the lowest tax rate — from 6.545% to 6.20% in 2001, the average of which (6.37%) will apply for 2000.

- Ontario reduces its middle-income tax rate from 10.01% to 9.24%, the average of which (9.62%) will apply in 2000. Note that while this reduction corresponds to the reduction in the federal rate from 26% to 24% (multiplied by 38.5%), Ontario effectively calls this an Ontario tax cut, as is arguably appropriate under a tax-on-income approach. However, readers may wish to view it as a "pass-through" of the federal tax cut to the Ontario tax system.

- Ontario effectively converts its two surtaxes, 20% of Ontario tax beyond $3,466 and an additional 36.91% of Ontario tax above $4,373, into two further tax brackets: 13.39% and 17.41% (when the former is 20% above the top rate of 11.16 and the latter is 36% above 13.39%).

- Finally, Ontario indicates that it will return to the tax on income in the next budget, and in particular, will rethink the tax structure including the surtax.

Ontario also proposed important cuts to its corporate tax rates — the general corporate rate of 15.5% and the manufacturing and processing rate of 13.5% will, in steps, both be lowered to 8%. The small business tax rate will be reduced from 8%, again in steps, to 4%, along with a doubling of eligible

Table 3: Ontario and Tax on Income

	Pre-2000 Tax Environment		
Taxable Income Brackets	*$29,590*	*$59,180*	
Federal Tax Rates	*17%*	*26%*	*29%*
Ontario tax rates before Ontario 1996 budget (equivalent to Ontario tax-on-tax rate of 58%)	9.86%	15.08%	16.82%
Ontario tax rates before Ontario 1999 budget (equivalent to Ontario tax-on-tax rate of 40.5%)	6.885%	10.53%	11.745%
Ontario tax rates after Ontario 1999 budget (equivalent to Ontario tax-on-tax rate of 38.5%)	6.545%	10.01%	11.165%
	2000 Tax Year		
Taxable Income Brackets	*$30,004*	*$60,009*	
Federal Tax Rates	*17%*	*25%*	*29%*
Ontario tax rates for 2000	6.37%	9.62%	11.16%
	2001 Tax Year		
Ontario tax rates for 2001 (tax brackets to be adjusted for inflation)	6.20%	9.24%	11.16%

Note: Ontario also has two surtaxes: a 20% tax on Ontario tax in excess of $3,466 plus 36% on tax in excess of $4,373. In effect, this will create two further tax brackets: 13.39% and 17.41%.

taxable income from $200,000 to $400,000. Anticipating some of the ensuing analysis, Finance Minister Eves commented as follows on the reductions in the general and manufacturing/processing tax cuts:

> this will be the lowest general corporate income tax in Canada. When our tax cut plan is fully in place, the combined Ontario and federal corporate income tax rate would also be more than 10 percentage points lower than the average rate of the US Great Lakes States, our biggest competitors for businesses and jobs. (Eves, 2000a, p. 26)

Another issue that will come up later relates to the attempts by provinces to redefine income for tax purposes. Reference has already been made to Saskatchewan's proposal to assess all farm-related capital gains at the lowest marginal tax rate. Along similar lines, Ontario proposes to reduce the inclusion rate for capital gains from 75% to 66% for year 2000. This would parallel the 2000 federal budget proposal. However, in 2001 Ontario would decrease the inclusion rate to 62%, and eventually to 50% by 2004. This amounts to a different definition for taxable income than that adopted by Ottawa. This would also apply to Ontario's proposals for stock options and for flow-through shares. Finance Minister Eves offers the following view of these provisions:

> Ontario enters into this new tax-on-income system with the expectation of full policy flexibility. The measures proposed in this Budget have no meaningful administrative impediments to their implementation. There should be no reason that the Canada Customs and Revenue Agency could not administer these measures as proposed. However, Ontario is prepared to administer its own tax policy initiatives if the federal government fails to cooperate for the benefit of all taxpayers. (Eves, 2000b, p. 70)

Thus, one of the issues that will merit attention in the following section is whether or not the tax collection agreements will survive the shift from tax on tax to tax on income.

Quebec

Quebec established its own PIT tax collection system in the mid-1950s. Thus, it has long had full rate-and-bracket flexibility as well as the freedom (within constitutional limits) to define income for tax purposes. Therefore, Quebec's personal income tax was *unaffected* by Ottawa's changes in tax rates and indexing in the 2000 federal budget. Quebec is different from the other provinces in another way as well. In the 1960s Quebec opted to receive some of its transfers from Ottawa in the form of an additional tax-point transfer rather than in the form of cash. These 16.5 tax points are usually referred to as the "Quebec abatement". The remaining nine provinces chose to retain cash transfers. In what follows, I shall present the Quebec tax rates both including and excluding the abatement.

Prior to its 2000 budget, Quebec's rate and bracket structure was as follows: 20% up to $25,000; 23% between $25,000 and $50,000; and 26% beyond $50,000. As Table 4 indicates, the 2000 Quebec budget (after altering the thresholds slightly) lowers these three rates for year 2000 to 19%, 22.5% and 25% respectively. By 2002 the rates will have fallen to 17%, 22% and 24% respectively. And from 2002 onward, full indexation will apply.

The final column in Table 4 represents my attempt to present Quebec tax rates in a manner consistent with the tax-on-income rates for the other provinces. To do this, I transfer the 16.5 tax points (the Quebec abatement) back to Ottawa. This abatement equals 2.805% for the 17% federal rate (i.e., 16.5% of 17%); 3.96% for the federal middle-income tax rate (16.5% of 24%) and 4.785% for the top federal rate (16.5% of 29%). If one subtracts these abatements from Quebec's tax rates, this should place the Quebec rates on the same basis as those of the other provinces. Another way to view this is that the abatement transfers these percentages from the federal to the Quebec tax system. What my calculation does is transfer them back to Ottawa, that is, it restores the 17-24-29 federal tax rate. As the final column of Table 4 indicates, subtracting these abatements from Quebec's legislated tax rates for 2001 yields the tax-on-income equivalent tax rate of 15.185%, 18.54% and 20.215%.

Not only are these arguably the highest rates of all provinces, but the thresholds for the middle- and upper-income brackets are also much lower. One has to be careful with these comparisons, especially at the low-income level since not only does Quebec have a generous family policy, but as the last row of Table 4 indicates, it converts the personal and spousal exemptions into tax credits at a high tax rate, even if one allows for the abatement.

Table 4: Quebec Tax Rates

	Before Budget	After Budget			Comparable Rates (2001)*
		2000	*2001*	*2002*	
		(percent)			
Tax Table					
Taxable income brackets					
0 to $25,000 $25,000 to $26,000	20 23	19	18	17	15.185
$26,000 to $50,000 $50,000 to $52,000	23 26	22.5	22.5	22	18.54
52,000 +	26	25	25	24	20.215
Rate used to calculate tax credits	23	22	21.5	21	

Note: *Quebec's rates placed on a comparable basis with other provinces (see text for details).

This completes my *tour d'horizon* of provincial responses to the 2000 federal budget. I now turn to some of the implications as they relate to intergovernmental relations, both federal-provincial and interprovincial.

The 2000 Budgets and Fiscal Federalism

The rate and bracket flexibility under the new tax-on-income approach substantially enhances the provinces' room to manoeuvre on the taxation front. Future changes to federal rates, brackets, indexation and even the value of non-refundable credits will no longer influence provincial tax systems. Thus, along with greater flexibility will come greater provincial accountability, since the provinces will not be able to blame Ottawa for changes in their provincial tax systems. Moreover, the system will become more transparent. Applying a rate and bracket structure against taxable income is much more comprehensible to citizens than a single provincial tax levied against federal tax owing, replete with a set of cascading surcharges. Likewise, cross-province comparisons will become much more transparent which will, in turn, surely heighten the degree of cross-province competition (e.g., the Saskatchewan response to Alberta's single-rate tax).

To be sure, this shift to tax-on-income was not the creation of the 2000 budget, it was in the works since the federal-provincial finance ministers conference in December of 1997. Nonetheless, the 2000 federal budget not only served as the catalyst for triggering the immediate shift to a tax-on-income by several provinces but, as well, served to influence the nature of the provincial tax-on-income systems. As noted earlier, Ottawa's decision to focus its up-front tax cuts more towards achieving social equity has effectively transformed much of the responsibility for generating competitive income taxation systems to the provinces. While I remain a fan of competitive federalism as it relates to the tax system, I also believe that Ottawa should take the lead in ensuring that the income taxation of mobile factors is internationally competitive. As a result, the provinces are taking significant tax initiatives in order to maintain and grow their economic bases. For example, the rhetoric underlying the recent series of Ontario tax cuts and Alberta's single-rate tax is embedded in competitiveness concerns. Among the ways in which the consequent evolution of income taxation may affect fiscal federalism are the following:

- Not all provinces feel the same competitive pressure or are of a philosophical persuasion to reduce taxes on mobile factors. This will, I think, lead to an increased divergence in top marginal tax rates across provinces. The data in the previous section appear to point in this direction — a top marginal rate in Alberta of 10.5% and a top rate in Quebec in 2001 of nearly twice this (i.e., 20.215%, from Table 4). Neither Quebec nor Alberta have surcharges so that comparing the top marginal rates is straightforward. However, the comparison across the provinces that do have them (the remaining provinces except Saskatchewan) is more complex and in any event many of these provinces will be rethinking these surtaxes in their future budgets.

- But even in the unlikely event that the pre-2000 budget disparity in top marginal rates does not widen, the sensitivity of mobile factors to tax advantages appears to have heightened. Thus, there looms the prospect of diverging growth rates across provinces, with Toronto, Calgary and (likely soon) Vancouver emerging as the focal points for attracting mobile talent and human capital.

- While all provinces (except Nova Scotia) are actively engaged in reducing personal and corporate taxes, the two richest provinces (Ontario and Alberta) have cut their tax rates the most. Should the British Columbia Liberal Party (with its dramatic tax proposals) win the next election, then the three "have provinces" would combine to trigger a sharp fall in the equalization standard (via a fall in the national average tax rate). Moreover, since its budget, Alberta is moving to match Ontario's cuts on the corporate tax front. The intriguing, although highly problematical, result could be increasing absolute and relative per capita revenues in the have provinces alongside a decrease in equalization.

The above three points basically address issues of horizontal fiscal balance. However, the concerns related to these likely-increasing imbalances trigger some further and more problematic implications:

- Given that the rate-and-bracket freedom under tax on income places all provinces on a par with Quebec, it does not take much imagination to predict that several of the provinces will be eager to make the systems even more comparable. In short, Ontario, among others, will request the 16.5 additional personal income tax points that Quebec now has. Ottawa will deny the request. But this refusal will feed into the following two issues.

- Suppose that the significant lowering of corporate and personal income taxes in, say, Alberta and Ontario leads to a substantial increase in economic activity. The tax revenue benefits of this activity uptick will now accrue more to Ottawa than to Ontario and Alberta, in comparison with the mid-1990s, for example, since Ottawa's tax rates are relatively higher than they were previously. This will worsen the existing fiscal imbalance between Ottawa and the provinces, the result of which will be that the provinces will increase pressure on the federal government for personal and corporate income tax cuts.

- The much more serious implication is the following. Again consider Ontario and assume that the province still feels a competitive need to reduce income taxes but cannot afford the revenue cost of further cuts. What does it do? It begins to tamper with the definitions of income for tax purposes, which is, of course, exactly what Ontario did in its 2000 budget. Its proposals include redefining income as it relates to capital gains, certain types of stock options, and selected flow-through share programs. Moreover, as noted above Ontario fully expects the new Canada Customs and Revenue Agency (CCRA) to administer its tax system with those provisions included. If Ottawa refuses, then Ontario apparently stands ready to mount its own collection system.

Perhaps the implications have already gone too far. It would admittedly be a stretch to imply a direct link between an Ontario withdrawal from the tax collection agreements and the failure to have more personal and corporate income tax relief for mobile factors in the 2000 federal budget. It may be preferable to come at this from the other direction. Had Ottawa devoted more attention in recent budgets to ensuring that our income tax systems, personal and corporate, were competitive within a North American context, the system would presumably now be characterized by a smaller divergence in marginal tax rates across provinces, a better federal-provincial fiscal balance and fewer tensions on the tax collection agreement front.

Postscript: The October 18, 2000 Mini-Budget

While it is normal for the minister of finance to present an economic statement in October, this year's *Economic Statement and Budget Update 2000* was anything but normal. One reason for this is that there has been a seismic shift in the underlying budget parameters over the period from the February 2000 federal budget to the October 18, 2000 *Economic Statement*. For example, the February budget estimated the surplus for fiscal year 1999-2000 to be $5.5 billion. One would have expected this to be a reasonably accurate estimate of the surplus since the fiscal year-end (March 31, 2000), however, was barely a month after the budget. When the final data for the fiscal year became available (fall 2000) the surplus turned out to be $12.3 billion. Even more dramatic, the projected cumulative budget surpluses over 2000-01 to 2005-06 are forecast in the *Economic Statement* to be in excess of $120 billion, and this already incorporates the Table 2 tax-rate reductions.

A second reason is that the *Economic Statement and Budget Update* also serves as the tax and debt planks of the Chrétien Liberals' platform for the November 27, 2000 election. More to the point, this mini-budget incorporates a further substantial round of tax cuts. Admittedly, the possibility exists that the Liberals could be defeated at the polls and, therefore, the provisions of the *Economic Statement* would never see the light of legislated day. Nonetheless, they merit highlight since the *Economic Statement* is appropriately viewed as the latest instalment of the tax reform process that began with the February budget.

For both of these reasons it is important to focus on the highlights of this *Economic Statement*, albeit almost as a postscript rather than an integrated analysis.

Continuing with Tax Reform

The *Economic Statement's* approach to tax reform is a combination of accelerating the implementation of the five-year plan as shown in Table 1 and of providing further tax cuts for Canadians. All of the proposed tax cuts listed below are to be in effect as of January 1, 2001. The provisions include:

- reducing the lowest tax rate from 17% to 16%;
- reducing the 24% tax rate (which was reduced in the 2000 budget from 26%) to 22%;
- adding a new tax bracket for incomes between $60,000 and $100,000 which will have a rate of 26%. Alternatively, this can be viewed as reducing the top marginal tax rate from 29% to 26% for incomes between $60,000 and $100,000;
- maintaining the top marginal rate of 29% for incomes above $100,000;
- abolishing the federal surtax;
- reducing the capital gains inclusion rate from the 66.67% in the 2000 budget to 50%;
- introducing more generous rules for stock options and flow-through shares;
- establishing the timetable for corporate tax cuts proposed in the 2000 budget (see Table 1). The legislated cut from 28% to 27% on January 1, 2001 will remain. The rate will then fall progressively to 25% (on January 1, 2002), to 23% (on January 1, 2003) and finally to 21% (on January 1, 2004).

These are very significant tax cuts in their own right and they merit further highlight.

The first point to note about these tax reductions is that many of them relate to unfinished business pertaining to the February 2000 federal budget. For example, this mini-budget addresses those provisions of the five-year tax reform plan (see Table 1) that were not already addressed in Table 2, for example, the schedule for corporate tax reductions and the abolition of the federal surtax. Essentially, this is the *acceleration* component of the February budget's tax reform plan.

Second, beyond completing this unfinished business, there is a further round of substantial tax reductions. Of and by itself, this is not surprising given the magnitude of the projected surpluses. What is surprising are the income-distributional implications of these tax reductions. Specifically, in light of the above analysis I would have assumed that the finance minister would have taken advantage of the massive surpluses to reduce the tax rates on mobile factors. Admittedly, Paul Martin did remove the 5% surtax immediately. However, the corporate tax reductions are implemented gradually in spite of the rather minimal costs of pursuing an aggressive first-mover advantage over the Americans. Nonetheless, when fully implemented, Canadian corporate rates will be lower than U.S. corporate rates.

All of the new (i.e., not in Table 1) tax reductions are geared to low- and middle-income Canadians: only the top marginal tax rate remains unchanged, while the other rates are lowered. Some of this may relate to electoral politics. Just prior to the election call, the Canadian Alliance converted their 17% single-rate tax into a two-rate version — 17% up to $100,000 and 25% thereafter. In this light, the mini-budget's reduction of the lowest tax rate from 17% to 16% is presumably an attempt to "one-better" the Alliance, as it were. Moreover, the reduction of tax rates for those under $100,000 allows the Liberals to claim that they are generous to low- and middle-income Canadians but not to high-income Canadians, that is, the 16% to 29% tax-rate range compared to the 17% to 25% range of the Canadian Alliance scheme allows the Liberals to claim the "progressivity" high ground. Presumably, this is where they wish to position themselves politically. But I also think that this is where they want to position themselves ideologically. Hence, it is tempting and I think appropriate to argue that they have not bought into the reality that globalization requires lower rates on highly mobile Canadians.

But there is another way, a quite sophisticated way, that one might rationalize their new four-tiered rate structure — 16%-22%-26%-29%. It would go as follows. Not only should the personal income tax be a progressive tax, but the progressivity should come primarily from the federal rate and bracket structure. This view would certainly have been nurtured by Alberta's move to a flat tax or single-rate tax for its PIT. If Ottawa were to flatten its rate structure, and if other provinces were to attempt to follow Alberta's example, the resulting rate and bracket structure might embody very little in the way of progressivity. But this is not appropriate for a personal income tax system, or so the argument would go. Therefore, the only way that the federal government can ensure that the PIT will be a progressive tax is to embody progressivity in its own portion of the tax. And why not *increase* the degree of progressivity in the context of generally reducing tax rates.

This is a very different approach to PIT reform than the one I proffered above, namely that Ottawa should take the lead role in ensuring that our tax rates on mobile factors are competitive. Given, however, that Ottawa has re-affirmed its intent to ensure that its component of the PIT is oriented towards income-distributional goals rather than competitive goals, this becomes in effect an invitation for the provinces to follow Alberta's flat-tax approach. Even Albertans with their 10.5% single rate tax will face a rather progressive tax system overall — 0% until the federal exemption is reached; 16% until the larger Alberta exemptions are used up; 26.5% up to $30,000; 32.5% between $30,000 and $60,000; 36.5% from $60,000 to $100,000; and 39.5% thereafter. Under the former tax-on-tax approach to the shared PIT, the provinces were forced to *magnify* the progressivity imposed by Ottawa, since they were required to levy a single tax against federal tax owing. They are now free to decide for themselves the degree of progressivity they wish. By increasing the progressivity of its own component, Ottawa is effectively ensuring that the overall PIT system will remain progressive. At the same time, however, it is probably providing an *incentive* for provinces, especially those with mobile tax bases, to follow Alberta's lead and to opt for relatively flat-tax structures.

Could this be part of the rationale for the increase in federal progressivity in the mini-budget? My answer is that it could, but not without an important caveat: it is the federal government, with its large surpluses, and not the provinces, that can afford to reduce top marginal rates. Thus, under this general scenario, high marginal tax rates on mobile knowledge workers will remain in place because the provinces (except for Alberta) do not have the fiscal flexibility to reduce them to competitive levels. This cannot be the end of the story.

The Tax Collection Agreements

Earlier in the analysis, I noted that Ontario was proposing to alter the definitions of income for Ontario tax purposes in three areas: capital gains, stock options and flow-through shares. And if the CCRA then refused to collect Ontario's taxes, the province threatened to establish its own PIT collection system. This is in the nature of a credible threat, so that it should perhaps not be surprising that the mini-budget addresses all three of these areas. In terms of the capital gains inclusion rate, it adopts the Ontario 50% rate. The remaining provisions relating to stock options and flow-through shares may not address directly the Ontario concerns, but they are certainly "in the neighbourhood", as it were. With these provisions, Ontario's threat to withdraw from the tax collection agreements is no longer credible. This, too, is unlikely to be the end of the story. Indeed the two stories are related. Stay tuned.

References

Alberta Tax Review Committee (1998), *Future Directions for Personal Income Taxes in Alberta*, Final Report and Recommendations (Edmonton: Alberta Treasury).

Courchene, T.J. (2000), "A Paul Martin, Sr. Budget", *Policy Options/Options Politiques* 21(3), 17-20.

Eves, Finance Minister E. (2000a), *Balanced Budgets: Brighter Futures: Ontario Budget 2000, Budget Speech* (Toronto: Queen's Printer for Ontario).

__________ (2000b), *Balanced Budgets: Brighter Futures: Ontario Budget 2000, Budget Papers* (Toronto: Queen's Printer for Ontario).

Martin, the Honourable P. (2000a), *Better Finances, Better Lives: The Budget Plan 2000* (Ottawa: Finance Canada).

__________ (2000b), *Economic Statement and Budget Update 2000* (Ottawa: Finance Canada).

Saskatchewan Personal Income Tax Review Committee (1999), *Final Report and Recommendations* (Regina: Government of Saskatchewan).

Session Two
THE BUDGET AND ITS MACROECONOMIC EFFECTS

MACROECONOMIC EFFECTS OF BUDGET 2000

Thomas A. Wilson, Peter Dungan and Steve Murphy, University of Toronto

Introduction

The February 2000 federal budget provides an extensive package of tax reductions and new spending initiatives. Taken together the measures included in the budget provide a net fiscal stimulus of $7.4 billion in 2000-01, increasing to $10 billion in 2001-02, and $12.3 billion in 2002-03.

As in the past, the analysis of the federal budget is complicated by two factors.

- As in previous budgets, the budget "back-loads" a significant amount of spending into the expiring fiscal year (1999-2000). As the prospective surplus was quite large this year, $4.5 billion of spending initiatives booked to fiscal 1999-2000 were possible, while applying the $3 billion contingency reserve to debt reduction.

- Several spending and tax initiatives were announced prior to the budget, either late in 1999 or early in 2000. On the tax side there was a 15¢ reduction in the employee Employment Insurance (EI) rate (with a corresponding 21¢ reduction in employer rate) and some small increases in tobacco taxes. On balance these tax measures would reduce revenue by about $0.3 billion in 1999-2000, and by $1 billion in fiscal 2000-01. On the spending side, there were a variety of initiatives, adding up to $1.4 billion in 1999-2000 and $1.1 billion in 2000-01.

Like previous Martin budgets, the 2000 budget presents a two-year fiscal plan (but provides revenue and expenditure estimates for three years). A "planning surplus" is developed by combining the $3 billion contingency reserve with economic "prudence" factors of $1 billion for fiscal 2000-01 and $2 billion for fiscal 2001-02. For planning purposes, EI payroll tax reduction of 10¢ per year are also projected.

However, this budget represents a major departure from recent practice in presenting a five-year tax reduction plan. While this plan is a statement of intent, rather than a firm commitment, and the timing of future tax cuts is not spelled out, the presentation of even a tentative medium-term tax reduction plan will hopefully improve future fiscal planning within government. It will represent a yardstick against which future budgets will be judged. Our analysis of this five-year plan is presented later in the paper.

We organize the presentation of our analysis of the economic and fiscal effects of the budget as follows. We present two sets of estimates: one for the budget measures alone (excluding projected EI rate cuts), and the other for the budget measures combined with the tax and spending initiatives implemented prior to the budget as well as prospective EI payroll tax cuts over the next three years. We refer to the second set of measures as the "augmented budget". In all model runs, we allow for impacts on provincial revenues and assume that the Bank of Canada will neutralize any impacts of the fiscal stimulus on either prices or the exchange rate.

Impact Analysis of the Budget: Budget Measures Alone

Table 1 summarizes the tax and expenditure initiatives introduced in the 2000 budget over the next three fiscal years and shows how we have allocated the back-loaded spending across these years. Note that we have

Table 1: Total Federal Budget Impacts ($ million) (Budget Alone)

	2000-01	2001-02	2002-03
Revenue			
Personal			
Increase Credits	-420	-730	-1,145
Cut middle rate, increase brackets	-1,955	-2,925	-3,490
Cut Surtax	-185	-305	-330
Other Personal*	-290	-680	-910
Total Personal	-2,850	-4,640	-5,875
Corporate			
Rate Cuts	-80	-465	-520
Other	+75	+75	-25
Total Corporate	-5	-390	-545
TOTAL REVENUE IMPACTS	-2,855	-5,030	-6,420
Spending			
Transfers to Provinces**	1,000	500	500
Transfers to Persons	33	643	997
International Aid	285	155	200
Infrastructure	300	550	750
Goods & Services	2,449	2,105	2,086
Child Tax Benefit	475	1,020	1,350
TOTAL SPENDING IMPACTS	4,542	4,973	5,883
Total Budget Impacts	-7,397	-10,003	-12,303

Notes: * Includes GST adjustment ($15m in 2000-01, $40m in 2001-02, $45m in 2002-03).

** Provinces are assumed to spend the money on goods and services.

moved the Child Tax Benefit to the spending side of the budget, since this measure is treated (properly) as a transfer payment in the National Accounts.

For fiscal 2000-01, once the allocated back-loaded spending initiatives are taken into account, spending increases total $4.5 billion, while tax reductions are $2.9 billion, for a total fiscal impulse of $7.4 billion. In fiscal 2001-02, tax reductions increase substantially to $5 billion, slightly higher than the spending increases that year. By the third fiscal year, when the full effect of the tax reductions are felt, tax reductions total $6.3 billion, and spending increases $5.8 billion. (Note that all figures cited are relative to base, not to the previous year.)

We implement all of the spending increases in the budget as changes to exogenous variables in the FOCUS model. The general changes in tax rates and indexing are implemented by changing appropriate parameters in the tax equations of the model. All other tax changes are accommodated by add-factors.

Two changes will affect the provinces during the calendar year 2000. As provincial taxes (outside Quebec) remain tied to federal "basic tax" via the current "tax-on-tax" system, indexing and the reduction in the middle bracket rate will reduce provincial revenues this year. We assume that the provinces do not react to the reduction in their revenues — that is, provincial budget balances are reduced, and the tax reductions augment households' disposable income. Next year we assume that all provinces will de-couple their taxes from the federal tax, replacing the tax-on-tax system with separate provincial rate schedules. We assume that all provinces will index their personal income taxes.

The magnitude of the fiscal stimulus provided by the budget measures is shown in Table 2, which presents the economic and fiscal effects with monetary policy neutralizing the exchange rate effect. As is apparent, the budget would provide a significant stimulus to real aggregate demand, with the real gross domestic product (GDP) up 0.6 - 0.8% over the three-year period. However, this stimulus would gradually build up inflationary pressures, with the price level increased by 1% by the third year, and with inflation up 0.5%.

Table 2: Federal Budget Impacts
Budget Measures only - Target Base Exchange Rate
(Impacts are percentage changes unless otherwise indicated)

	2000-01	*2001-02*	*2002-03*
Real Output and Components			
Real Gross Domestic Product	0.61	0.81	0.68
Consumption	0.64	2.00	3.00
Government Current and Capital	1.70	1.09	0.65
Residential Construction	0.43	0.66	0.60
Non-Residential Construction	-0.04	-0.69	-2.11
Machinery and Equipment	0.05	-0.70	-2.50
Exports	-0.04	-0.25	-0.64
Imports	0.38	1.06	1.48
Prices, Wages and Unemployment			
Implicit Deflator for GDP	0.08	0.45	1.02
Consumer Price Index	0.09	0.45	0.97
CPI - Inflation Rate (% pts)	0.10	0.36	0.53
Average Wage	0.17	0.66	1.31
Employment	0.26	0.62	0.73
Unemployment Rate (% pts)	-0.17	-0.38	-0.41
Interest Rates, Exchange Rate and Balance of Payments			
90-day Paper Rate (% pts)	0.21	0.55	0.70
Industrial Bond Rate (% pts)	0.21	0.56	0.72
Exchange Rate	0.00	0.00	0.00
Current Account Balance ($ bill)	-2.20	-6.42	-10.61
Deficits and Debt			
Aggregate Surplus/Deficit ($ bill)	-6.17	-6.55	-7.37
Federal Surplus/Deficit ($ bill)	-6.26	-8.37	-10.83
Ratio of Federal Debt to GDP (% pts)	0.09	0.60	1.30
Prov'l Surplus/Deficit ($ bill)	-0.01	1.52	2.99

With the current economic forecast outlook, it is appropriate to assume, therefore, that the Bank of Canada would act to offset these inflationary pressures. The second set of estimates, reported in Table 3, shows the economic effects when the central bank acts to neutralize the impacts of the fiscal stimulus on prices.

With this monetary policy, the aggregate demand effects are more modest, with real output increasing by only 0.1% in 2001-02 and by 0.4% in 2002-03. The required monetary restraints leads to an increase of interest rates of about 0.5%, and an appreciation of the dollar of just over 1%. With the aggregate demand effects somewhat tamed, the effects of the budget on the composition of demand are emphasized. As is clear, the budget measures (combined with the monetary restraint) shift the composition of demand towards consumption and government spending, and away from investment and net exports. The negative effects on investment are due to the increase in interest rates which swamps the effects of the 1% reduction in the corporate tax rate. With the negative effect on net exports, the current account balance declines by about $10 billion by the third year.

Under this scenario, the fiscal effects of the budget measures are increased. This reflects the effects of higher interest rates on the public debt (and the cumulative effect of reduced surpluses on debt-service charges). There is a small negative effect on the fiscal position of the provinces, which largely attenuates by the third year.

Impact Analysis of the Budget: Budget Measures Augmented with Pre-budget Spending and Tax Changes and Projected EI Payroll Tax Cuts

As noted in the introduction, there were some spending initiatives adopted after the November Statement, but before the budget. There was also a 15 cent EI payroll tax cut on January 1, 2000 and small increases in tobacco taxes. The budget tables include the planning assumption that future EI payroll tax cuts of 10 cents will occur at the beginning of the next three calendar years.

Table 3: Federal Budget Impacts
Budget Measures only - Target Base CPI
(Impacts are percentage changes unless otherwise indicated)

	2000-01	*2001-02*	*2002-03*
Real Output and Components			
Real Gross Domestic Product	0.05	0.11	0.37
Consumption	0.58	1.73	2.59
Government Current and Capital	1.79	1.47	1.48
Residential Construction	-1.83	-2.40	-1.12
Non-Residential Construction	-1.23	-2.46	-2.99
Machinery and Equipment	-1.05	-3.06	-4.31
Exports	-0.44	-0.84	-1.15
Imports	0.54	0.71	0.76
Prices, Wages and Unemployment			
Implicit Deflator for GDP	0.03	0.04	0.06
Consumer Price Index	0.03	0.00	0.00
CPI - Inflation Rate (% pts)	0.03	-0.03	0.00
Average Wage	-0.03	-0.02	0.07
Employment	0.06	0.16	0.32
Unemployment Rate (% pts)	-0.04	-0.10	-0.20
Interest Rates, Exchange Rate and Balance of Payments			
90-day Paper Rate (% pts)	0.53	0.66	0.52
Industrial Bond Rate (% pts)	0.54	0.67	0.54
Exchange Rate	0.63	1.06	1.21
Current Account Balance ($ bill)	-4.10	-7.24	-10.23
Deficits and Debt			
Aggregate Surplus/Deficit ($ bill)	-9.20	-12.36	-13.99
Federal Surplus/Deficit ($ bill)	-8.35	-11.76	-14.00
Ratio of Federal Debt to GDP (% pts)	0.45	1.42	2.48
Prov'l Surplus/Deficit ($ bill)	-0.88	-0.68	-0.20

Table 4 summarizes the tax and expenditure changes which comprise this "augmented budget". Tables 5 and 6 present our analysis of the economic effects of the augmented budget under the two different monetary policy assumptions. As the results in Table 5 reveal, if monetary policy neutralizes the exchange rate effects, there are stronger real demand effects than those shown in Table 2. As well, the demand stimulus results in a price level increase by 1% by the third year, with the inflation rate increasing to 0.6%.

We therefore focus our attention on Table 6, which presents the economic and fiscal effects when the Bank of Canada neutralizes the impact of the fiscal policies on prices. Not surprisingly, the augmented budget has somewhat stronger real output effects than the budget alone. This is mainly a result of the favourable supply side-effects generated by the payroll tax cuts. With the direct downward pressure on labour costs from the reduction in employer payroll taxes offsetting some of the inflationary demand pressures, a higher level of output is consistent with zero net inflationary effects.

The pattern of changes in the composition of demand is similar to that of Table 3, but with the positive effects on consumption somewhat stronger, as are the negative effects on investment and net exports. The net fiscal effects on the federal budget are again increased by the impact of higher interest rates on debt-servicing costs. However, except for a small decline in the first year, provincial budget balances show a modest improvement in this scenario.

Updating Forecasts: A Word of Caution

The previous two sections have provided standard impact analyses of the economic and fiscal effects of the 2000 budget. However, as is well known, these results only have predictive value if the fiscal initiatives were wholly unanticipated. Since most, if not all, economic forecasters had incorporated some fiscal stimulus in their forecasts prior to the budget, the results presented in the previous section cannot simply be added to the forecasts to derive a post-budget forecast.

Table 4: Total Federal Budget Impacts ($ million)
(Augmented Budget)

	2000-01	*2001-02*	*2002-03*
Revenue			
Personal			
Increase Credits	-420	-730	-1,145
Cut middle rate, increase brackets	-1,955	-2,925	-3,490
Cut Surtax	-185	-305	-330
Tobacco Excise Tax	+70	+70	+70
Other Personal*	-290	-680	-910
Total Personal	-2,780	-4,570	-5,805
Corporate			
Rate Cuts	-80	-465	-520
Tobacco Surtax	+70	+70	+70
Other	+75	+75	-25
Total Corporate	+65	-320	-475
EI Rate Cuts	-1,392	-2,175	-2,980
TOTAL REVENUE IMPACTS	-4,107	-7,065	-9,260
Spending			
Transfers to Provinces**	1,000	500	500
Transfers to Persons	544	1,143	997
International Aid	285	155	200
Infrastructure	300	550	750
Goods & Services	3,035	2,325	2,306
Child Tax Benefit	475	1,020	1,350
TOTAL SPENDING IMPACTS	+5,639	+5,693	+6,103
Total Budget Impacts	-9,746	-12,758	-15,363

Notes: * Includes GST adjustment ($15m in 2000-01, $40m in 2001-02, $45m in 2002-03).
** Provinces are assumed to spend the money on goods and services.

Table 5: Federal Budget Impacts
Augmented Budget Measures - Target Base Exchange Rate
(Impacts are percentage changes unless otherwise indicated)

	2000-01	*2001-02*	*2002-03*
Real Output and Components			
Real Gross Domestic Product	0.87	1.23	1.07
Consumption	0.89	2.70	4.00
Government Current and Capital	1.99	1.14	0.56
Residential Construction	0.80	1.27	1.10
Non-Residential Construction	0.13	-0.50	-2.32
Machinery and Equipment	0.18	-0.54	-2.75
Exports	0.02	-0.16	-0.62
Imports	0.42	1.32	1.91
Prices, Wages and Unemployment			
Implicit Deflator for GDP	-0.01	0.38	1.08
Consumer Price Index	0.01	0.36	1.00
CPI - Inflation Rate (% pts)	0.02	0.36	0.64
Average Wage	0.20	0.83	1.69
Employment	0.39	0.94	1.13
Unemployment Rate (% pts)	-0.26	-0.57	-0.63
Interest Rates, Exchange Rate and Balance of Payments			
90-day Paper Rate (% pts)	0.23	0.67	0.89
Industrial Bond Rate (% pts)	0.23	0.68	0.91
Exchange Rate	0.00	0.00	0.00
Current Account Balance ($ bill)	-2.31	-7.45	-12.73
Deficits and Debt			
Aggregate Surplus/Deficit ($ bill)	-7.50	-7.19	-7.78
Federal Surplus/Deficit ($ bill)	-8.06	-10.26	-13.16
Ratio of Federal Debt to GDP (% pts)	0.15	0.76	1.61
Prov'l Surplus/Deficit ($ bill)	0.46	2.69	4.73

Table 6: Federal Budget Impacts
Augmented Budget Measures - Target Base CPI
(Impacts are percentage changes unless otherwise indicated)

	2000-01	*2001-02*	*2002-03*
Real Output and Components			
Real Gross Domestic Product	0.42	0.50	0.46
Consumption	0.84	2.46	3.58
Government Current and Capital	2.06	1.50	1.41
Residential Construction	-1.03	-2.13	-1.74
Non-Residential Construction	-0.83	-2.35	-3.89
Machinery and Equipment	-0.68	-2.82	-5.03
Exports	-0.30	-0.76	-1.34
Imports	0.57	1.02	1.37
Prices, Wages and Unemployment			
Implicit Deflator for GDP	-0.04	0.01	0.13
Consumer Price Index	-0.05	-0.04	0.01
CPI - Inflation Rate (% pts)	-0.04	0.00	0.05
Average Wage	0.04	0.19	0.37
Employment	0.24	0.49	0.63
Unemployment Rate (% pts)	-0.15	-0.30	-0.36
Interest Rates, Exchange Rate and Balance of Payments			
90-day Paper Rate (% pts)	0.50	0.81	0.95
Industrial Bond Rate (% pts)	0.51	0.84	0.98
Exchange Rate	0.50	1.01	1.63
Current Account Balance ($ bill)	-3.93	-8.52	-13.74
Deficits and Debt			
Aggregate Surplus/Deficit ($ bill)	-9.92	-13.03	-15.91
Federal Surplus/Deficit ($ bill)	-9.73	-13.78	-17.36
Ratio of Federal Debt to GDP (% pts)	0.43	1.55	2.90
Prov'l Surplus/Deficit ($ bill)	-0.24	0.57	1.11

The PEAP forecast prepared prior to the budget, for example, had allowed for significant tax reductions and program spending increases over the next three years. On the tax side, we had anticipated personal income tax (PIT) surtax reductions which closely approximated those in the budget, and had assumed that indexing would be restored on January 1, 2001 (one year later than the budget) but we did not fully anticipate the timing of the middle bracket rate cut. We did anticipate the general corporate rate decrease next year, and expected (and continue to expect) similar cuts in each of the next few years (although the depth of the proposed total corporate rate cuts in the budget surprised us). Prior to the budget, we had assumed EI rate cuts of 15¢ per year, and we have carried over this assumption to our post-budget forecast.

It is difficult to do a close comparison for program spending because our model is on a National Accounts basis, and because substantial revisions to the National Accounts expenditure numbers were included in the preliminary annual estimates released at the end of February. If we simply compare federal program spending levels in our pre- and post-budget forecasts, program spending is about $1.1 billion higher in 2000-01, about $2.1 billion higher in fiscal 2001-02, and about $2.3 billion higher in fiscal 2002-03. These changes are much smaller than these shown in Tables 1 and 4.

Because we had incorporated most of the fiscal stimulus provided in the budget, the effects of incorporating the budget measures into our latest forecast are relatively small, and are swamped by the combined effects of past data revisions and the strength of the economy revealed in recent data.

Looking Ahead to the Medium Term: The Five-Year Tax Reduction Plan

This section presents our analysis of the five-year tax reduction plan. Since the likely time pattern of future specific tax cuts was not specified in the Budget 2000 document, we assume that future tax reductions are implemented gradually over the next four years.

As the five-year plan did not specify further spending increases, we have initially projected most spending components on the basis of inflation plus population growth. The three exceptions are old age pensions (which are based on demographics and inflation), employment insurance benefits (which are based on the number of unemployed and average wages), and transfers to the provinces (which are based on existing federal-provincial arrangements).

The five-year analysis differs from the impact analysis presented earlier. As a comparison base, we use a model solution in which the surplus is held at $3 billion (Public Accounts basis) and the remaining potential surplus or fiscal dividend is exhausted through tax-free transfers to persons. This approach, which was the basis of the fiscal dividend measurement exercise last fall, has the advantage that we do not start from a base case involving unrealistically high future surpluses. Over the medium term the issue is not about fiscal impacts, but rather about the appropriate allocation of the fiscal dividend. This approach, coupled with the assumption that the Bank of Canada will neutralize any price effects, virtually eliminates any major aggregate demand effects. It focuses instead on the supply-side effects of the allocation of the fiscal dividend.

As noted earlier, while the ultimate targets for tax reduction in 2004-05 are presented, the time pattern of specific tax reductions is not specified (except for EI payroll tax cuts). However, a table on p. 84 of Budget 2000 provides estimates of the time patterns for the three major revenue sources (PIT, corporate income tax and EI contributions) which indicates that the bulk of the income tax cuts occurs in the final year. However, as the minister of finance and his officials have indicated that this represents the *absolute minimum* tax reduction over the five-year period, we assume that the future tax reductions will be spread out over the period.

In this analysis we assume a reasonably steady pattern of tax reductions, with the exception that the additional 1% point reduction in the middle bracket rate is implemented on January 1, 2002. The timing and magnitude of the tax reductions (relative to base) are shown in Table 7. When the future tax reductions are added to those implemented with the augmented budget, by the fifth year the annual amount of the tax reductions is $19.5 billion.

Table 7: Total Federal Budget Impacts ($ million)
(Augmented Budget - Remaining Tax Cuts Implemented Smoothly to 2004-05)

	2000-01	*2001-02*	*2002-03*	*2003-04*	*2004-05*
Revenue					
Personal					
Increase Credits	-420	-730	-1,145	-1,796	-2,760
Cut middle rate, increase brackets	-1,955	-4,149	-5,391	-6,461	-7,270
Cut Surtax	-185	-350	-520	-750	-865
Tobacco Excise Tax	+70	+70	+70	+70	+70
Other Personal*	-290	-680	-910	-1,080	-1,325
Total Personal	-2,780	-5,839	-7,896	-10,017	-12,150
Corporate					
Rate Cuts	-80	-500	-1,400	-2,200	-2,995
Tobacco Surtax	+70	+70	+70	+70	+70
Other	+75	+75	-25	-25	-25
Total Corporate	+65	-355	-1,355	-2,245	-2,950
EI Rate Cuts	-1,392	-2,175	-2,980	-3,786	-4,391
TOTAL REVENUE IMPACTS	-4,107	-8,369	-12,231	-16,048	-19,491
Spending					
Transfers to Provinces**	1,000	500	500	500	0
Transfers to Persons	544	1,143	997	997	997
International Aid	285	155	200	200	200
Infrastructure	300	550	750	750	750
Goods & Services	3,035	2,325	2,306	2,115	1,845
Child Tax Benefit	475	1,020	1,350	1,680	2,525
TOTAL SPENDING IMPACTS	+5,639	+5,693	+6,103	+6,242	+6,317
Total Budget Impacts	-9,746	-14,062	-18,334	-22,290	-25,808

Notes: * Includes GST adjustment ($15m in 2000-01, $40m in 2001-02, $45m thereafter).
** Provinces are assumed to spend the money on goods and services.

As a starting point for the analysis we have set the debt-reduction target for each year at $3 billion (PA basis). This involves a National Accounts surplus of $6-6.5 billion each year. We programmed the model to adjust spending (on non-taxable transfers) each year so as to be consistent with the tax-reduction and debt-reduction targets. The value of these non-taxable transfers provides an estimate of the remaining "fiscal dividend".

As noted above, the base case for this analysis is a model solution with the same $3 billion annual debt-reduction target, and with future program spending increasing roughly in line with population growth and inflation[1] (with the remainder of any potential surplus expended through increased transfers to persons).

With the Bank of Canada neutralizing the price level effects, aggregate real demand effects will be small and transitory. The results are primarily indicative of the supply-side impact of the strategy, as well as the impact on the composition of demand. Finally, the analytical results will yield an estimate of potential future surpluses or fiscal dividends which take into account any favourable supply-side effects of the tax-reduction package.

Table 8 shows the economic effects of the Budget 2000 allocation of the fiscal dividend. As is apparent, there are modest increases in real output, reflecting the favourable supply-side effect of reductions in payroll taxes and corporate taxes. By the fifth year, real output is increased by 0.3%, with employment and productivity growth each accounting for 0.15%.

The composition of demand is shifted towards investment and net exports. The favourable supply-side effects of the budget package permit an easier monetary policy, with lower interest rates and a somewhat lower exchange rate.

---

[1]Expenditure projections through fiscal year 2002-03 are based on Budget 2000 estimates. Future spending on transfers to the provinces reflect current policies. Old Age Security and EI benefit payments are generated by the FOCUS model. All other program spending components are projected on the basis of population growth plus inflation.

Table 8: Allocating the Fiscal Dividend: Effects of Implementing the Five-Year Tax-Reduction Plan
(Impacts are percentage changes unless otherwise indicated)

	2000-01	*2001-02*	*2002-03*	*2003-04*	*2004-05*
Real Output and Components					
Real Gross Domestic Product	0.41	0.30	0.22	0.21	0.31
Consumption	-0.42	-0.65	-0.68	-0.76	-0.72
Government Current and Capital	2.04	1.45	1.38	1.18	0.75
Residential Construction	0.98	1.44	0.63	0.23	0.58
Non-Residential Construction	0.53	1.10	1.18	1.36	2.12
Machinery and Equipment	0.44	1.04	1.25	1.05	1.52
Exports	0.15	0.30	0.33	0.41	0.52
Imports	-0.06	0.00	0.08	-0.10	-0.11
Prices, Productivity and Employment					
Implicit Deflator for GDP	-0.08	-0.05	0.01	-0.01	0.00
Consumer Price Index	-0.06	-0.04	0.02	-0.01	-0.01
Labour Productivity	0.22	0.02	-0.02	0.04	0.15
Employment	0.20	0.28	0.23	0.16	0.16
Unemployment Rate (% pts)	-0.13	-0.17	-0.12	-0.06	-0.05
Profits and Capital Formation					
Pre-Tax Corporate Profits	2.34	1.37	1.16	1.29	1.85
Capital Stock	0.02	0.10	0.23	0.34	0.45
Interest Rates					
90-day Paper Rate (% pts)	-0.05	-0.08	-0.02	-0.13	-0.20
Industrial Bond Rate (% pts)	-0.05	-0.08	-0.02	-0.13	-0.21
Exchange Rate and Balance of Payments					
Exchange Rate	-0.15	-0.30	-0.35	-0.45	-0.55
Current Account Balance ($ bill)	0.28	0.82	0.73	1.81	2.44
Deficits and Debt					
Aggregate Surplus/Deficit ($ bill)	1.40	1.76	1.51	1.13	1.72
Federal Surplus/Deficit ($ bill)	0.93	1.23	1.03	0.85	1.32
Ratio of Federal Debt to GDP (% pts)	-0.19	-0.28	-0.36	-0.40	-0.49

This allocation of the fiscal dividend has favourable effects on the budget balance. As a result of lower interest rates and higher tax revenues from stronger growth, the annual budget surplus is increased by $0.9 to $1.3 billion. Over the five-year period, the debt-GDP ratio declines by 0.5 percentage points.

Table 9 presents our analysis of the size of the fiscal dividend over the five-year period. As shown, even with the smooth implementation of the five-year tax reduction plan, the budget measures do not exhaust the fiscal dividend. When the additional budget surpluses generated by the budget package are taken into account, moreover, the surpluses are increased.

When the direct and indirect effects of the budget are factored in, there is a substantial residual fiscal dividend of about $12 billion in fiscal year 2004-05. The magnitude of these potential surpluses suggests not only that the smooth implementation of the five-year tax-reduction plan is feasible, but also that we can anticipate additional tax reductions in future budgets.

Table 9: Estimate of the Fiscal Dividend ($ billion)
(After allowing for the $3 billion annual contingency reserve to be applied to debt reduction)

	2000-01	*2001-02*	*2002-03*	*2003-04*	*2004-05*
Pre-budget estimate	9.7	13.5	19.0	26.1	32.5
Ex ante post-budget estimate	4.3	3.3	4.3	7.0	10.8
Ex post post-budget estimate*	5.2	5.5	5.3	7.9	12.1

Note: * This estimate includes the favourable fiscal effects shown in Table 8.

Conclusions

Over the near term, Budget 2000 provides a modest fiscal stimulus to real output. Real output could increase by as much as 0.6 to 0.8% if monetary policy targets the exchange rate. In the more likely case where monetary policy targets the inflation rate, however, the real output stimulus is only 0.1 to 0.4%.

In our view, the medium-term consequences of the budget are more important than these short-run effects. The restoration of full indexation will reduce the automatic upward drift of personal income tax burdens. The five-year tax-reduction plan represents the beginning of a process that should lead to a tax structure more conducive to efficiency and growth. Budget 2000 has charted the course towards these ends, and has implemented the initial steps. Future budgets should not only meet the commitments of the five-year plan, but also move beyond it to meaningful reforms of the personal and corporate income tax systems.

MACROECONOMIC EFFECTS OF THE 2000 FEDERAL BUDGET

Rick Egelton, Bank of Montreal

After years of restrictive federal budgets, the improved fiscal position of the federal government has given the fiscal authorities something they haven't experienced in many years: choice. The government has the option of applying the projected fiscal surpluses to reducing the debt, increasing program spending, tax relief or some combination thereof. The course of action taken by the government has implications for economic growth, financial markets and inflation. This paper examines the macroeconomic effects of the February 2000 federal budget.

The impact of the budget on the economy depends primarily on four key factors:

- the size of the fiscal stimulus;
- the impact, if any, on potential output;
- the degree of excess capacity in the Canadian economy; and
- the response of the Bank of Canada.

Size of the Fiscal Stimulus

The magnitude of the fiscal stimulus directly impacts demand in the economy. Figure 1 approximates the net fiscal impulse of the 2000 federal

Figure 1: Fiscal Impulse
(Change in the cyclically-adjusted primary federal balance, Public Accounts basis)

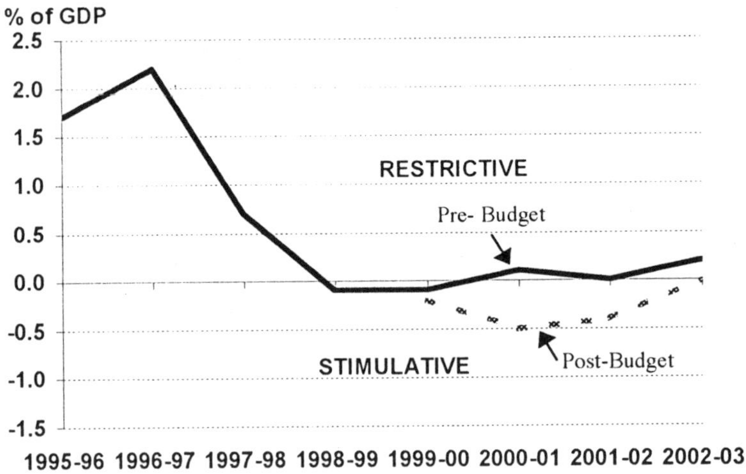

Source: Department of Finance and Bank of Montreal.

budget by examining the change in the cyclically-adjusted primary federal balance as a share of gross domestic product (GDP), both pre and post the 2000 budget. We have modified the cyclically-adjusted primary balance to smooth the lump sum expenditures booked in 1996-97 ($800 million Foundation for Innovation), 1997-98 ($2.5 billion Millennium Scholarship Fund), 1998-99 ($3.5 billion Canada Health and Social Transfer [CHST] payment) and 1999-2000 ($2.5 CHST transfer and additional $900 million in Foundation for Innovation) to reflect when the expenditures will actually be made. To the extent that the cyclically-adjusted primary balance is falling as a share of GDP, fiscal policy can be said to be expansionary. The converse is true during years in which the cyclically-adjusted primary balance is rising as a share of GDP.

Figure 1 suggests that federal fiscal policy was very restrictive in the 1995-97 period, directly subtracting around 1.5% of GDP from growth on average. Fiscal policy has been basically neutral in 1998 and 1999 and the status quo fiscal stance (pre-2000 budget) is estimated to be slightly restrictive for the 2000-02 period. The tax cuts and program spending initiatives contained in the 2000 budget have rendered the fiscal stance stimulative in 2000 and 2001 by almost 0.5% of GDP per year and effectively neutral in 2002.

The closer the economy is operating to capacity, the less the impact of the fiscal stimulus on growth. The reason is straightforward. If the economy is operating at potential, the fiscal stimulus will create excess demand conditions leading to higher inflation with no lasting impact on the level of output. Conversely, if there is a considerable output gap, there will be only a limited impact on inflation and the fiscal stimulus raises the level of output by an amount equal to the fiscal stimulus plus the second round effect of increased demand on employment and subsequently, on spending.

Impact on Potential Growth

The budget is likely to have very little impact on potential growth, at least through 2002. First, many of the budget measures — like increased defence spending — while perhaps necessary, will not increase the capacity of the economy to produce goods and services. Of the $33.6 billion in spending and tax initiatives contained in the budget, roughly 44% will have virtually no impact on potential output. Budget initiatives that will likely have an impact on potential output — municipal infrastructure improvements, encouraging research and innovation and personal and corporate tax cuts — are of a longer term structural nature, having little impact on potential output by the year 2002.

Figure 2: Unemployment Rate

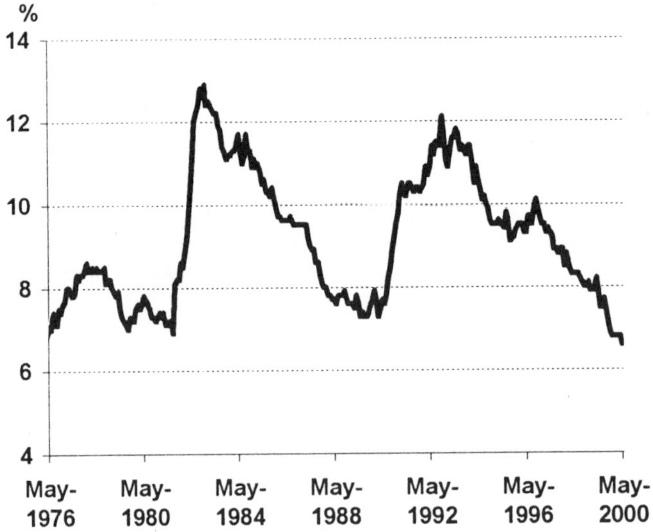

Source: Statistics Canada.

Figure 3: Output Gap

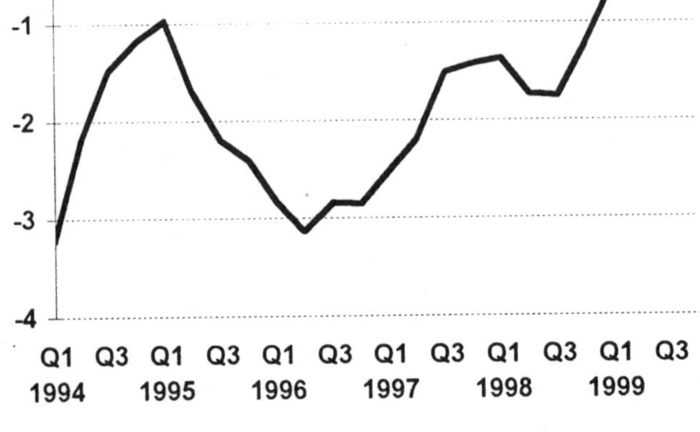

Source: Bank of Canada.

Degree of Excess Capacity

By most conventional measures the Canadian economy is operating quite close to, or even at, its capacity limits: the unemployment rate of 6.6% is at its lowest rate in more than 20 years; industrial capacity utilization rates are at cyclically high levels; and the Bank of Canada's measure of the output gap suggests that the economy is now in an excess demand situation. Moreover, growth over the past several quarters has been quite strong and should continue at an above-potential pace, at least through the third quarter. This suggests that any fiscal stimulus will simply generate increased price pressures and have only a transitory impact on the level of output.

On the other hand, there is reason to believe that conventional measures may understate the amount of excess capacity in the economy. First, the behaviour of wage and price inflation is not indicative of an economy operating at its potential level of output. Core inflation remains mired near the bottom of the Bank of Canada's 1-3% inflation target band while wage cost increases continue to be very subdued. Second, labour force participation rates are well below pre-1991 peaks, whereas in the United States participation rates are at all-time highs. This suggests that improved labour markets may induce previously discouraged workers back into the labour force, providing the economy with some additional room to grow before labour markets become excessively tight. Finally, the U.S. experience would seem to indicate that, for whatever reason, the natural rate of unemployment is likely below estimates that economists believed possible only a few years ago. Perhaps the same is true for Canada.

Response of the Bank of Canada

Monetary policy holds the key as to whether the fiscal stimulus will have any material impact on economic growth. In an environment of inflation targeting, the Bank of Canada essentially works backwards from its inflation target to an implicit growth target that will be necessary to achieve the inflation target. Monetary conditions are then set to achieve the growth objectives. Therefore, assuming that monetary conditions are set at levels designed to achieve a particular growth and inflation path prior to the budget, a stimulative fiscal stance will raise projections for real growth to above desired rates.

As a result, the Bank of Canada will tighten monetary conditions to keep the real growth and inflation outlook at its pre-budget path. The fiscal stimulus would therefore have no lasting impact on real growth and inflation. However, it will result in monetary conditions, interest rates and the exchange rate, being tighter than under the status quo fiscal stance. This is particularly the case in an environment in which growth is clearly above potential and the economy, according to estimates from the central bank, is operating at capacity.

Bottom Line

While the 2000 federal budget provides some fiscal stimulus for this year and next, its impact on economic growth will be minimal at best, reflecting a correspondingly tighter monetary stance from the Bank of Canada. The tighter monetary stance means that, *ceteris paribus*, interest rates and the exchange rate will be higher. This will shift the composition of growth away from exports and interest-sensitive categories of demand-like business investment and housing, towards government and consumer spending on non-durable goods and services.

The monetary offset is expected for two reasons: first, with growth above potential and the output gap largely closed, any stimulus to growth will need to be offset by tighter monetary conditions in order to avoid higher inflation. Second, with inflation targeting, the central bank implicitly must also target a desired path for GDP growth. Thus, any stimulus to growth from looser fiscal policy must necessarily be offset by tighter monetary policy in order to keep growth on track and achieve the Bank's inflation target.

Two caveats are in order here. First, as mentioned earlier the Canadian economy may be further away from capacity constraints than is generally believed. This would allow the Bank of Canada to accommodate the fiscal stimulus. Second, while the Bank of Canada officially targets inflation, the conduct of monetary policy is often swayed by movements in the value of the Canadian dollar. This explains, to some extent, why inflation has consistently been below the mid-point of the Bank's inflation target band since the inception of inflation targeting in 1991. Thus, if monetary policy is currently tighter than desired in order to support the value of the Canadian dollar, then it does not follow that the Bank of Canada would need to offset the fiscal stimulus. Under these conditions, the 2000 budget could positively impact real growth in 2000 and 2001.

MACROECONOMIC FORECASTS AND THE BUDGET

Gregor Smith, Queen's University

For macroeconomists, one of the key questions about the 2000 federal budget is: What would be the effects of faster debt reduction? Advocates of debt reduction emphasize the importance of saving for a rainy day. They argue that reducing debt may allow more room for fiscal policy to be used in stabilization, when the next recession arrives.

The other reason for interest in debt reduction is that it may boost national savings. The forecasts presented by Thomas Wilson, Peter Dungan and Steve Murphy show the budget's fiscal stimulus leading to declines in the current account balance and in investment, which are worrying signs for growth. Inverting their predictions means that debt reduction would raise these measures of national wealth accumulation. In the 1980s and 1990s, many Canadian macroeconomists were convinced that higher public saving would lead to higher national saving (Do you remember the "twin deficits"?). Ricardians were scarce. Formal models which assessed the effect of budget deficits on saving included those of Macklem, Rose and Tetlow (1994), James (1994) and Scarth (1999). There is no reason why this effect stops when the deficit passes through zero on the way to surplus, yet for some reason the case for public saving has not had a large impact. One reason seems to be that the public, as studied in opinion polls, thinks that fiscal prudence requires only a balanced budget, regardless of past deficits. But that may beg the question of why this view is so widespread.

Some commentators argue that debt reduction is not worth trying because it does not lead to a rapid fall in the debt-to-GDP ratio. The problem with their argument is that they take the path of gross domestic product (GDP) as given whereas it is endogenous. If debt reduction raises savings and growth, then it may lead to faster declines in the ratio than simple arithmetic on the numerator would suggest.

A second macroeconomic question suggested by the budget is: What is the effect of the tilt in the composition of federal spending? The last several budgets have featured a trend to new spending on education and research, for example through the Canada Foundation for Innovation. The 2000 budget continued this trend. Macroeconomists would like to be able to predict the effects on growth of this change, but as far as I know there are no attempts to do so in Canada. Perhaps the Department of Finance has begun work to estimate this effect.

One of the striking developments in recent federal budgets has been the increasing reference to private sector macroeconomic forecasts. For example, Annex 5 to the 2000 budget allows us to insert forecasts for GDP and interest rates and see how sensitive the budget is to these predictions. Annex 5 even tells us how the responses of revenue and expenditure to GDP and interest rates have been changing over time, which is an admirable feature. Private sector forecasts may also play a role in monetary policy, as argued by Hall and Mankiw (1994), Svensson (1997), and Bernanke and Woodford (1997).

Given this role in policy, how do we evaluate the forecasts? Years ago, economists would painstakingly examine the entrails of large, macroeconomic models as a way to assess their usefulness. I think it is now recognized that this examination is not worthwhile. A good forecasting record may stem as much from good judgements by the forecasters as from a good model. Thus evaluation must be based on prediction errors. Ideally, we would hear from forecasters about the accuracy of their 1999 predictions before listening to their 2000 ones.

Naturally, to evaluate forecasts requires more than just the average prediction made by a group of forecasters. We need the complete panel to judge the records of individual firms and also because the dispersion may contain information. For example, policymakers may have more confidence in an average forecast if there is virtual unanimity than if the same average reflects widely different views that cancel each other. Presenting an average and calling it the "consensus" throws away this information.

Unfortunately, there is no Canadian macroeconomic forecasting tournament. A variety of institutions and firms, including Statistics Canada, the Conference Board, KPMG, the Department of Finance and Consensus Economics, collects some of the data required. While these efforts are valuable, none of them produces a panel adequate for statistical evaluation. Ideally, a tournament would feature a short list of variables to be forecasted, identical dates *at* and *for* which forecasts are made, and sharing of forecasts once they are submitted to the organization running the tournament. A good model for such a contest is the U.S. Blue Chip survey (www.bluechippubs .com) which has been conducted monthly for 23 years. Its U.S. forecasts are used by the Department of Finance in Canadian government budgeting.

I forecast that Canadian macroeconomic forecasters would readily participate in such a tournament. The costs of entering the forecasting industry are very low, so it is in the interest of established forecasters to differentiate themselves by advertising their track records in the only realm that matters: prediction.

References

Bernanke, B. and M. Woodford (1997), "Inflation Forecasts and Monetary Policy", *Journal of Money, Credit, and Banking* 29, 451-468.

Hall, R.E. and N.G. Mankiw (1994), "Nominal Income Targeting", in N.G. Mankiw (ed.), *Monetary Policy* (Chicago: University of Chicago Press).

James, S. (1994), "Debt Reduction with Distorting Taxes and Incomplete Ricardianism: A Computable General Equilibrium Analysis", in W. Robson and W. Scarth (eds.), *Deficit Reduction: What Pain, What Gain?* (Toronto: C.D. Howe Institute).

Macklem, R.T., D. Rose and R. Tetlow (1994), "Government Debt and Deficits in Canada: A Macro Simulation Analysis", in W. Robson and W. Scarth (eds.), *Deficit Reduction: What Pain, What Gain?* (Toronto: C.D. Howe Institute).

Scarth, W. (1999), "Alternatives for Raising Living Standards", mimeo, Department of Economics, McMaster University.

Svensson, L. (1997), "Inflation Forecast Targetting: Implementing and Monitoring Inflation Targets", *European Economic Review* 41, 1111-1146.

Session Three
THE TAXATION DIMENSION

COUNTING CHICKENS AND UNHATCHED EGGS: The Post-Budget Outlook for Canadian Taxes

William B.P. Robson, C.D. Howe Institute

Introduction: Chickens and Eggs

Going into its February 2000 budget, many observers hoped the federal government would address Canada's high tax burden with tax cuts that would be supportive of economic growth and reduce the uneven burdens that face similarly situated taxpayers. The budget responded with some immediate relief, and with more ambitious plans for future cuts.

In assessing the budget's impact, I divide the tax cuts it proposed into two types. The changes that took place immediately or are scheduled for implementation during the budget's projection period from fiscal year 1999-2000 to 2001-02 might reasonably be thought of as chickens that are safe to count. By contrast, the changes promised for the budget's "out years" — the period from 2002-03 to 2004-05 — are best thought of as eggs that may or may not hatch.

The former changes, the reasonably certain ones, are steps in the right direction, but only small ones. If fiscal policy through to 2004-05 follows the precedent of this budget and its immediate predecessors, with new spending — much of it in end-of-year binges — absorbing the bulk of discretionary fiscal room, lower marginal tax rates and greater fairness will remain largely elusive. Since this prospect is discouraging, I will close with some suggestions that might improve the chances that all the budget's eggs will produce healthy birds.

The Tax Challenge and the Budget's Response

The Challenge: Why We Needed Chickens

Although the past decade echoed with the language of government restraint, that restraint is not yet evident in Canadian taxes. Government revenues other than investment income stood at almost $13,000 per Canadian in 1999, up almost one-fifth in real terms from a decade earlier.[1] Relative to the economy, taxes took 41.5% of gross domestic product (GDP) in 1999, a barely perceptible drop from their all-time peak the previous year (Figure 1).

As a practical matter, high average rates of personal tax tend to mean very high effective marginal rates for taxpayers at some income levels, limiting the rewards from working and saving. They also tend to create major horizontal inequities, with similar discretionary family incomes attracting very different amounts of tax, depending on the number of earners and the presence of children.

On the business side, high tax rates undercut Canada's attractiveness as a place to produce goods and services. They also tend to amplify, indeed, they foster the creation of, differentials in the tax treatment of various sectors, a kind of industrial policy that, in Canada's case, tends to tilt against higher tech, service-oriented businesses that many Canadians look to for a richer, cleaner future.

---

[1]In this presentation, taxes are all government revenues on a National Accounts basis, less notional contributions to unfunded public service pension plans and return on investment (the latter adjusted to remove provincial government resource royalties).

Figure 1: Total Taxes in Canada in Relation to GDP

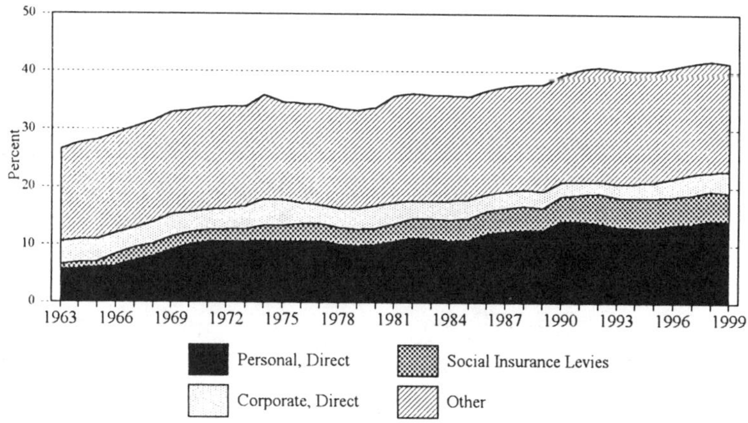

Although there is more than one layer of government in Canada, it seems fair to say that federal activity makes a key contribution to these problems. Looking at the share of personal money incomes taken by direct taxes, which is now over one-quarter on average, federal levies loom very large (Figure 2).[2]

With business taxes, matters are more complicated. There is no pronounced upward trend in the bite of direct taxes into the relevant base as there is on the personal side, and the federal share of the burden has declined somewhat (Figure 3), although the share of profits taxed is strikingly high for the boom phase of the business cycle. Moreover, direct taxes as measured in the National Accounts are only part of the story: they include federal capital taxes, but not provincial capital taxes or property taxes. Also important is that the business tax base is likely becoming more elastic, as the relative costs of transportation and communication shrink, the lure of the United States grows, and the number of jurisdictions that compete with Canada for investment increases. Last but certainly not least, the almost uniquely

---

[2]Money income is total income of the personal and unincorporated business sectors, less imputed rent on owner-occupied housing.

Figure 2: Personal Taxes and Social Insurance Levies as Share of Money Income

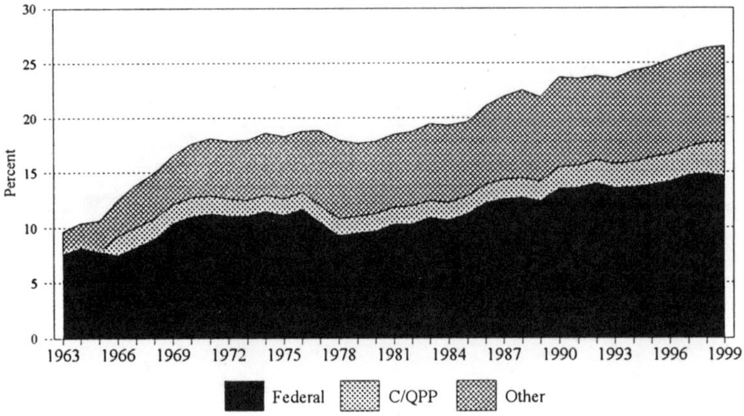

Figure 3: Direct Taxes on Corporations as Share of Pre-Tax Profits

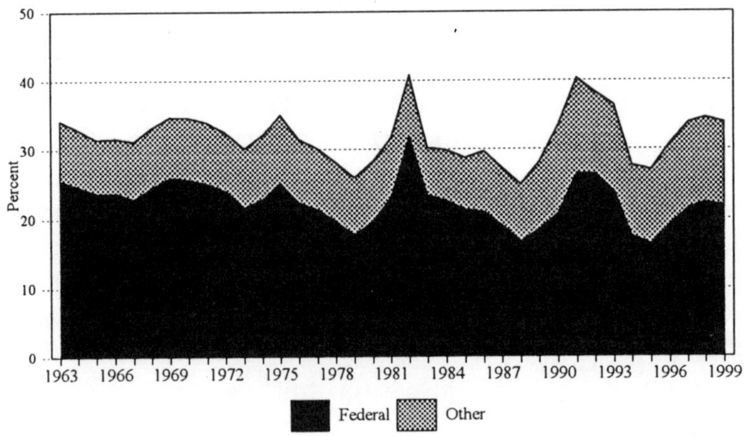

damaging effects of business taxes on incomes and growth make Ottawa's role in this area worthy of scrutiny as well.

What the Budget Produced

In the run-up to the budget, many commentators, including some at the C.D. Howe Institute (Robson, Mintz and Poschmann, 2000), urged Ottawa to address this situation. The case for federal action to cut taxes had three parts: Ottawa's turn around from unsustainable deficits to large incipient surpluses; the inevitability of higher Canada/Quebec Pension Plans levies following the much-needed 1998 reforms; and the fact that many provinces are already cutting taxes, but face pressure for health-care spending that make further sizeable, permanent cuts in their taxes unlikely. So we had a compelling combination of motive and opportunity in the pre-budget period, and the budget responded in a number of ways.

On the personal side, the budget promised to re-index personal income-tax thresholds to inflation, cut the middle rate from 26% to an effective 25% in 2000, and a promised 23% by 2004. It raised the threshold for the high-income surtax from $12,500 in federal tax to an effective $15,500 in 2000 and $18,500 thereafter, while dropping the rate to 4% for 2001 and promising to eliminate the surtax by 2004. It introduced more generous rules for medical expenses and attendant care, increased child-care deduction limits for people with disabled children, and raised tax-free limits for scholarships and bursaries. It lowered the inclusion rate for taxation of capital gains from three-quarters to two-thirds and, subject to qualifications, delayed capital gains taxes on stock options until they are exercised and allowed deferral on rollovers.[3]

On the business side, the budget lowered the general corporate income tax rate from 28% to 27% in 2001 — though not for resource companies or for "passive" business income — and promised to drop the rate to 21% by 2004. It raised the threshold for the preferential 21% tax rate for private Canadian-

---

[3]A significant change that does not fit easily into this list was the raising of the foreign investment limit in registered pension plans from 20 to 30%.

controlled corporations from $200,000 to $300,000 in 2001. And it increased capital-cost allowance rates and allowed for faster write-offs for certain types of producer durable equipment.

One way the budget claims, misleadingly, to cut taxes is by enhancing the child benefit. It also counts future increases in the child benefit and the goods and services (GST) tax credit arising from indexation of their amounts and clawback thresholds in its tax-cut total. But these are increases in transfer payments. Although Ottawa administers the child benefit and the GST credit through the tax system, that no more makes them tax cuts than delivering Employment Insurance (EI) benefits through the tax system would make them a tax cut. This misleading accounting deserves emphasis because these two programs together will soon exceed $10 billion annually (approximately equal to EI benefits), and evaluating Canadian taxes without them greatly understates both average and marginal tax rates.

Sorting the Chickens from the Eggs

How will these changes affect the overall burden of Canadian taxes, and some of the horizontal inequities and distortions I mentioned in describing the challenge? This question has a two-part answer, because the budget's proposals come in two flavours. There are the changes we can reasonably count on seeing because they are prefigured in detail in the projections for the next two years and will be part of the budget's implementing legislation: chickens we can safely count as hatched. And there are the proposals that are promised at some uncertain future date, and may not come to pass for various reasons: eggs laid by the budget that may simply stay eggs.

Chickens: The Outlook from 1999-2000 to 2001-02

For a look at the chicken-flavoured changes — those that will take effect in 2000 and 2001 — I will stay with the National Accounts basis presentation of the previous section. National Accounts figures are easier to interpret in a national and historical context, and also better capture the total impact of federal transactions on the country, because they record total taxes and transfers, rather than netting items such as the child benefit from revenues.[4] For projections of growth in the economy and various notional tax bases, I use forecasts for the next two years that yield nominal GDP growth similar to that in the budget projections.[5]

Over the next two years, the budget's changes promise an important drop in federal taxes measured against GDP (Figure 4). From the 1999s near-record 18%, they should drop by a bit more than a percentage point by 2001. This decline would leave them at their level of the late 1980s: years that in retrospect may appear to be a lower-tax era than they did at the time.

Turning to personal taxes — personal income taxes and EI levies[6] — the projected decline is less impressive (Figure 5). If money incomes grow in line with GDP over the next two years, the federal tax bite into money incomes should fall by slightly less than a percentage point. This decline seems rather small compared to the sizeable sounding numbers trumpeted in the budget, highlighting the fact that a hefty share of the budget's "tax-relief" total arises from reindexation, which does not cut tax rates but merely stops them rising, and from increases in the child benefit, which do not reduce total personal income tax collections. From this perspective, the burden of federal taxation will still be higher in 2001 than at any time before the early-1990s recession,

---

[4]This approach has the fault of requiring conversion of the budget projections into figures consistent with a National Accounts presentation. Among other things, this introduces the possibility of error by the converter. The figures presented here have been checked against data from the Department of Finance, but responsibility for errors is mine.

[5]I note in passing, however, that the forecasters surveyed by the Department of Finance appear to expect considerably faster growth of potential output per working-age Canadian in the future than in the recent past. They are correspondingly more optimistic about the prospects for sustained real growth being faster than 2.5% annually, with inflation staying below 2% annually, than I am myself.

[6]Like most analysts, I assume that the incidence of EI levies is on workers' incomes. Less defensibly, in this presentation, I treat the entire levy as a tax.

Figure 4: Federal Taxes Relative to GDP

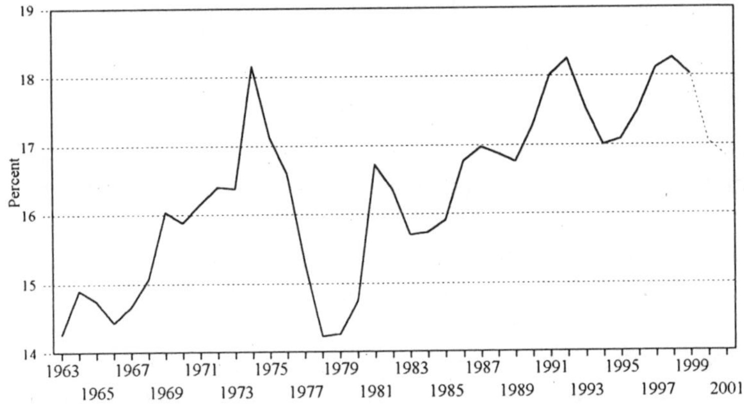

Figure 5: Federal Personal Taxes and EI Levies as Share of Money Income

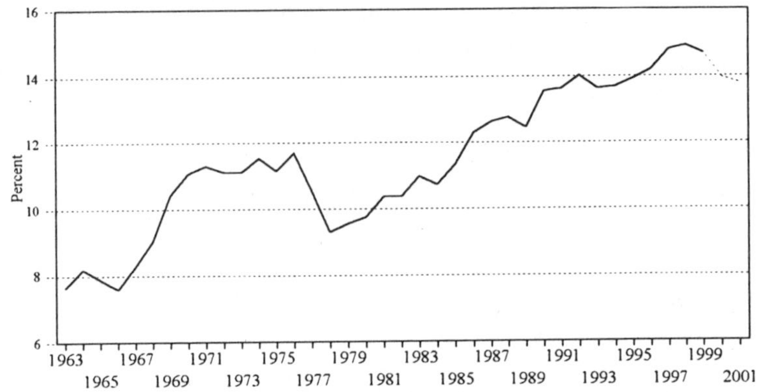

limiting the scope for lowering high marginal rates or lightening the load on Canadians who are disproportionately burdened.

On the business side, and assuming that corporate profits grow in line with GDP, the federal tax burden should fall by about 1.5 percentage points

(Figure 6). This is a step in the right direction, but not a decisive one — the share of profits taken by federal taxes normally swings with the cycle, but the recent tax load would be more suitable to a slump than the current expansion. If by 2001 the share of profits in GDP were to decline to its average level over the 1990s, reaping the revenue anticipated by the budget would require an effective tax rate around 27% — higher than in any year except 1982.[7]

Scratching Away at Personal Taxes

On the personal side, the relief in the 2000 budget is insufficient to produce decisive improvements in marginal tax rates facing individuals across the income scale.

Figure 6: Federal Direct Corporate Taxes as Share of Profits

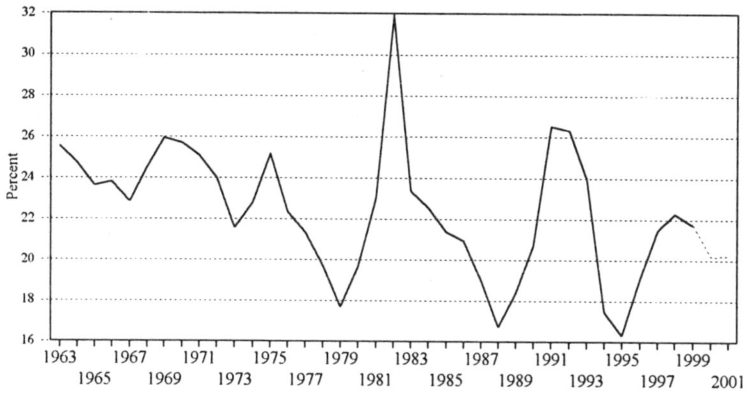

[7]Since federal corporate income tax revenue is a function of profits, this is an illustration, not a forecast. The budget's projections of rich collections from this source do raise questions about the wisdom of eliminating the economic prudence factors included in the November *Economic and Fiscal Update* from the budget projections to 2001-02.

Take, for example, a single-earner family with two children under the age of seven in Ontario. In 1999, the share of each additional dollar of earned income taken by governments through various levies and clawbacks rose rapidly as earnings approached the $30,000 mark, getting close to 70% at around $26,500 and again from $30,000 to $35,000 (Figure 7).[8] These marginal rates present a low-income person contemplating more or better-paid work to raise her/his living standards with a pretty powerful headwind. Provincial taxes and clawbacks are part of the problem, but Ottawa is the principal culprit, with clawbacks of the basic personal amount, the GST credit, the child benefit supplement and the child benefit stacking on top of regular income tax rates.

For such families with earnings higher than about $40,000, the 2000 budget represents part of a general pattern of improvement.[9] Lowering the middle rate reduces the government's share of each additional dollar earned through much of the relevant zone, and the 1999 budget's extension of the higher personal amount throughout the income scale also helps (as, for Ontario families, does the planned lowering of Ontario taxes).

For families with earnings from the low-to-mid-$20,000s to the high $30,000s, however, the 2000 budget's impact is not uniformly helpful. Focusing on the most problematic area, the more rapid clawback of a richer child benefit supplement pushes the federal effective marginal tax rate up by at least 4 percentage points in the range above $22,000, and by considerably more than that in the range above $27,000, where it overlaps with the clawback of the GST credit: adding provincial taxes and clawbacks would push the total effective marginal rate in this range over 70% in Ontario, which is not the worst province in this regard.

---

[8]These rates are calculated over $100 increments of earned income. I am grateful to Finn Poschmann for his indispensable collaboration in producing these figures.

[9]This illustration overstates the improvement slightly by using nominal dollars to compare 1999 with 2001 on the horizontal scale. Much of the movement of steps to the right simply reflects indexation.

Figure 7: Effective Marginal Tax Rates: Single-Earner, Two Kids in Ontario

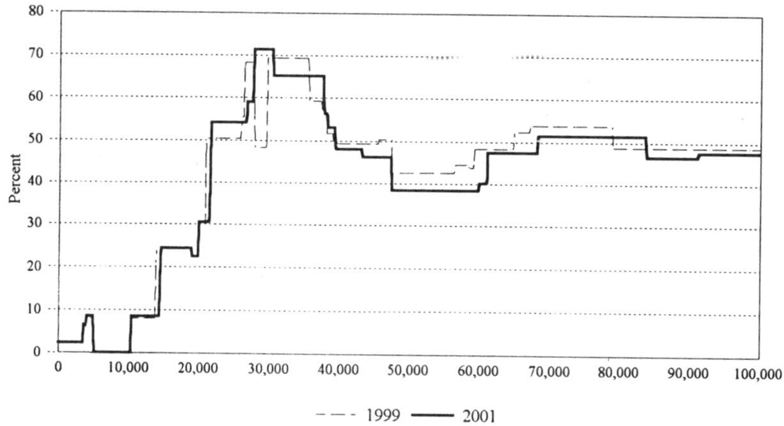

Two-earner couples are harder to describe, because producing a marginal rate progression schedule requires simplifying assumptions about the split of earnings that are open to objections. A simple before-and-after snapshot of a family with two children in Ontario whose earnings are split 60:40 nevertheless reveals a similar type of problem (Figure 8).

At higher income levels, the two-earner couple enjoys lower marginal rates, but the overlap of taxes and clawbacks means that, even with lower provincial taxes and EI premiums, marginal rates for these couples will be no lower, and sometimes appreciably higher, over the range from the high $20,000s all the way to the mid-$70,000s.[10]

Comparing the marginal rate progressions for one-earner and two-earner couples reveals an important contrast. Marginal rates for one-earner couples

---

[10]To facilitate comparison with the one-earner couple, the two earner couple is assumed to deduct child-care expenses of $2,000 per child, this being the level that several commentators (Boessenkool, 1999; Poschmann and Richards, 2000) have suggested for universal child deductions or credits.

Figure 8: Effective Marginal Tax Rates: Dual-Earner, Two Kids in Ontario

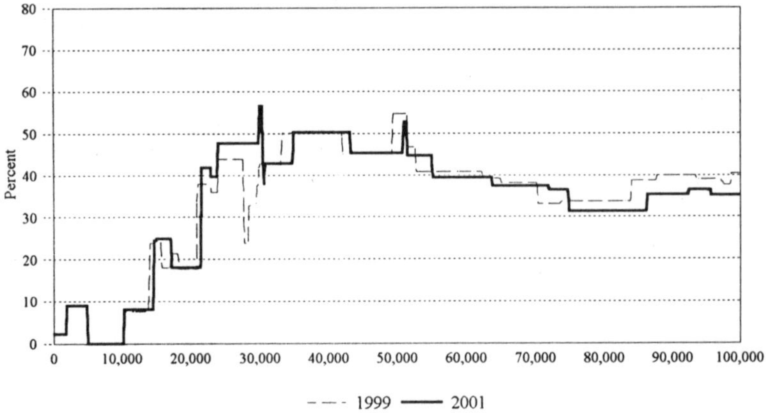

are, almost without exception,[11] higher than for two-earner couples until the two-earner couple hits its top marginal rate — which, for the 60:40 couple shown here, occurs at family income around $230,000 in 2001 (too far along the horizontal axis to be displayed in Figures 7 and 8 without losing interesting detail). This contrast means that one-earner couples pay more tax than two-earner couples with similar discretionary money incomes, and that the gap between the two family types rises with income (Figure 9).[12]

This discrepancy is usually justified, when it is justified at all, as an offset to the implicit income generated by a spouse in the home. In the absence of any consensus that the state should redistribute implicit income generated by living arrangements, however — let alone any accepted method for calculating such income — it seems regrettable that the unevenness in treatment of money incomes of different families will remain so stark in the budget's wake.

---

[11]In the 60:40 case, there is a span around $50,000 of family income where the two-earner couple faces the higher rate.

[12]As noted already, the two-earner couple's child-care expenses are capped at $2,000 per child in this illustration, to avoid exaggerating the contrast in discretionary income.

Figure 9: Total Taxes Payable, by Family Type
Two Kids in Ontario, 2001

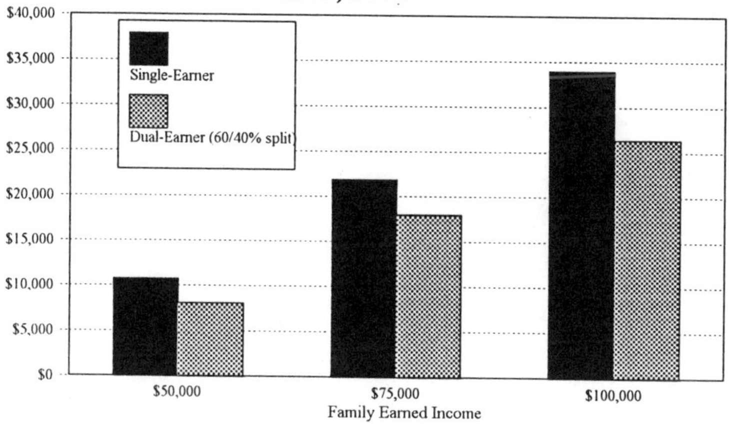

Note: Child-care expense deduction for dual-earner family limited to $2,000 per child.

Flying in the Face of Business Tax Imperatives

On the business side, the tax changes over the next two years are also helpful but hardly decisive. Thanks to business tax reforms in other developed countries, Canada's business tax rates now stand out as relatively unattractive. Even the full general corporate income tax rate cuts promised in the budget by 2004 would leave Canada's general rates above the current Organization for Economic Cooperation and Development (OECD) average (Mintz, 2000), let alone the lower OECD average likely to prevail in several years.

In the spirit of counting only chickens whose hatching we can confidently foretell, Figure 10 shows the marginal effective tax rates expected to prevail in 2001 on incremental capital investment by large, tax-paying firms in manufacturing and services respectively in the G7 countries, Sweden and Ireland.[13] In neither case does Canada stand out as particularly hospitable to new investment, and in services, the relative unattractiveness of Canada as a destination for new investment will still be stark.

---

[13]Source: International Taxation Program, University of Toronto. Figures for Canada are all-province averages. I thank Duanjie Chen and Jack Mintz for making these figures available to me.

Figure 10: Effective Tax Rate on Investment, 2001

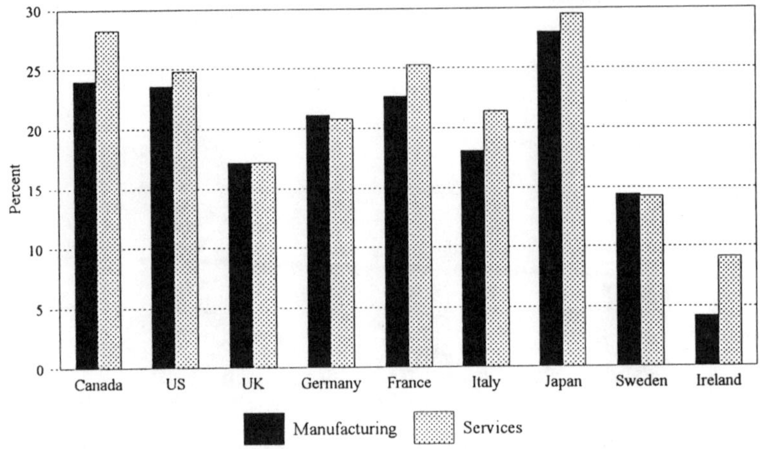

At least as important as average effective tax rates on new investment are the differences among the tax rates in different sectors (Figure 11). The budget promises to even out these differences, but they will remain substantial in 2001. Canada's tax system will still deviate markedly from the neutral treatment most economists would favour and, moreover, will not do so in the pro-"new economy" fashion that might find favour among advocates of growth-oriented industrial policy.

Will the Eggs Hatch?

To summarize to this point, the chickens we can confidently count following the 2000 budget are welcome, but they are outnumbered by unhatched eggs. What are the chances that some of the tax changes the budget promised but deferred for later — the reduction of the middle rate to 23%, the complete elimination of the personal surtax, and the lowering of general corporate tax rates — will actually come to pass? And can anything be done to improve these eggs' chances of hatching?

Figure 11: Effective Tax Rates on Investment by Sector, 2001

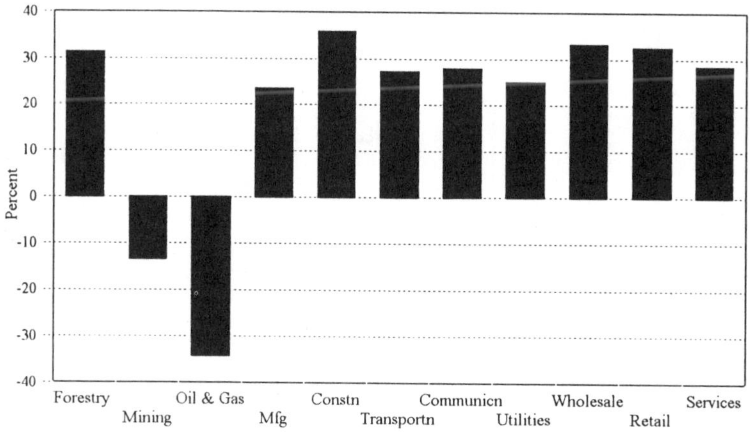

Hazards of a Long Incubation

To answer those questions, it helps to step back to the longer term projections of the November 1999 *Economic and Fiscal Update* (Canada, 1999b), and see how the room for fiscal manoeuvre outlined in that document looks in the budget's wake.

The November *Update* took average economic and fiscal projections from private sector forecasters and, assuming no policy changes, projected an "underlying surplus" adding up to $100.5 billion over the six years from fiscal 1999-2000 through to 2004-05. Of this amount, $72.5 billion arose during the second three years from 2002-03 to 2004-05, the budget's "out-years." The relevant numbers, and the revenue and spending projections underlying them, are shown in the top panel of Table 1.[14]

---

[14]The figures in Table 1 are on a Public Accounts basis. They are consistent with those in the November update, but show gross revenue and expenditure, rather than the net figures which, as discussed earlier understate the true impact of federal fiscal policy on Canadians (Robson, Mintz and Poschmann, 2000, p. 6).

Table 1: Summary of Federal Government Transactions, 1999-00 to 2004-05

	1999-00	*2000-01*	*2001-02*	*2002-03*	*2003-04*	*2004-05*	*1999/00-2001/02*	*2002/03-2004/05*	*1999/00-2004/05*
					$ billions				
November 1999 Fiscal Update									
Gross Taxes and Fees	165.6	172.7	180.9	188.4	196.5	205.5	519.2	590.4	1,109.6
Less Gross Program Spending	(123.7)	(126.4)	(131.2)	(134.2)	(137.3)	(140.8)	(381.4)	(412.2)	(793.6)
Less Net Debt Charges	(36.9)	(36.7)	(36.3)	(35.7)	(35.2)	(34.7)	(109.8)	(105.7)	(215.5)
Equals Underlying Balance	5.0	9.5	13.5	18.5	24.0	30.0	28.0	72.5	100.5
February 2000 Budget									
Gross Taxes and Fees	167.7	170.7	177.5	184.0	191.3	199.6	515.9	574.9	1,090.7
Less Gross Program Spending	(127.8)	(130.5)	(137.7)	(142.1)	(146.2)	(150.9)	(396.0)	(439.2)	(835.2)
Less Net Debt Charges	(36.9)	(37.2)	(36.8)	(36.2)	(35.7)	(35.2)	(110.8)	(107.2)	(218.0)
Equals Underlying Balance	3.0	3.0	3.0	5.7	9.4	13.4	9.0	28.5	37.5
Change from 1999 Update to 2000 Budget									
Gross Taxes and Fees	2.1	(2.0)	(3.4)	(4.4)	(5.1)	(5.9)	(3.3)	(15.5)	(18.9)
Gross Program Spending	4.1	4.0	6.6	7.8	9.0	10.1	14.7	27.0	41.6
Net Debt Charges	0.0	0.5	0.5	0.5	0.5	0.5	1.0	1.5	2.5
Underlying Balance	(2.0)	(6.5)	(10.5)	(12.8)	(14.6)	(16.6)	(19.0)	(44.0)	(63.0)

Updating those projections in the budget's wake involves three steps. First, I insert the budget's detailed projections for 2000-01 and 2001-02. Second, I project revenue and spending forward for the remaining years on the same basis as used in the *Update*, but with slightly lower revenue growth to account for reindexation. Third, I assume that unneeded economic prudence cushions will continue to be spent, since the 2000 budget continued the pattern of last-minute spending established by its predecessors.

The resulting new projections, shown in the middle panel of Table 1, give an underlying surplus for the 2002-03 to 2004-05 period of $28.5 billion. After deducting three years worth of contingency reserves, or $9 billion, this leaves $19.5 billion in discretionary room: a much diminished pot in which to find money both for further tax cuts and new spending.

The prospect that the government will actually use this fiscal room for tax cuts looks bleaker, moreover, in light of the outcome of the struggle between tax cuts and new spending that occurred after the publication of the November *Update* and the delivery of the 2000 budget. The first three years of the *Update's* projections, the years shown in detail in the budget, contained the other $28 billion of the $100.5 billion surplus projected over the full six years. In the budget's wake, the surplus over the first three years has dwindled to $9 billion: the total of the three years contingency reserves.

The bottom panel of Table 1 reconciles the *Update's* projections with the post-budget outlook, and shows what happened to the $19 billion difference. Higher debt-service charges took $1 billion: about one-twentieth. Lower revenue accounts for $3.3 billion: less than one-fifth. And higher program spending accounts for the remaining $14.7 billion: more than three-quarters of the difference. If tax cuts get a comparably small share of the surpluses from 2002-03 to 2004-05, most of the 2000 budget's remaining chickens will never see the light of day.

Helping the Chicks Emerge

It would be a shame if so many of the chickens promised in the 2000 budget remained just eggs. But there are steps that might improve their chances of hatching.

In my judgement, their chances would improve if Ottawa stopped highlighting net rather than gross tax and spending numbers in the Public Accounts. The growing importance of federal income support administered through the personal tax system makes the net numbers increasingly poor measures of the full scope and impact of Ottawa's activity. The Auditor General has called this presentation "incomplete financial disclosure",[15] and the government's response that this presentation "is consistent with the way Parliament appropriates funds" (Canada, 2000) is, in my view, hollow — Parliament only appropriates funds that way because the government presents the figures that way.

This debate matters for future tax relief: netting not only shrinks the apparent size of the federal tax burden at a point in time, it also lowers its apparent growth over time. Netting thus helps advocates of higher taxes and more spending argue that the federal government is shrinking to insignificance, an impression strikingly at odds with the reality facing most taxpayers.

A reinvigorated debate over tax reform could also help the chickens hatch. Personal taxes that are friendlier towards work and saving, and treat families with similar discretionary wealth more fairly, are worthy objectives. So are business taxes that enhance Canada's attractiveness as a place to invest, and treat different sectors more evenhandedly. Achieving these objectives is easier when governments can give up some revenue, making winners many and their winnings large, while keeping losers few and their losses small. Explicit commitments to lower personal tax rates and reduced inequities among families, and to a more attractive and less distorting investment climate, would hold out hope for higher living standards, and reinforce the will to preserve room for tax cuts in future budgets.

---

[15]Canada (1999a, p. 1.37). The Department of Finance deserves commendation for having included this discussion in the budget documents, despite its unsatisfactory response.

A Final Peep

In my view, the tax changes in the 2000 budget were steps in the right direction, but small ones. The chickens we can count are very welcome. But if Canadian taxes are to be more supportive of growth and are to be fairer by 2004, we need to make sure that the rest of the budget's chickens make it out of their shells.

References

Boessenkool, K. (1999), "Putting Tax Policy in its Place: How Social Policy Took Over the Tax Treatment of the Family", in D.W. Allen and J. Richards (eds.), *It Takes Two: The Family in Law and Finance* (Toronto: C.D. Howe Institute).

Canada (1999a), *Public Accounts of Canada 1999.* Volume 1: *Summary Report and Financial Statements* (Ottawa: Receiver General for Canada).

__________ (1999b), *The Economic and Fiscal Update: Translating Better Finances into Better Lives* (Ottawa: Department of Finance) November.

__________ (2000), *The Budget Plan* (Ottawa: Department of Finance) February.

Mintz, J. (2000), "The February 2000 Federal Budget's Business Tax Measures: Is Canada Missing the Boat?" Backgrounder (Toronto: C.D. Howe Institute).

Poschmann, F. and J. Richards (2000), *How to Lower Taxes and Improve Social Policy: A Case of Eating your Cake and Having It too,* Commentary (Toronto: C.D. Howe Institute).

Robson, W. (2000), "Nice Tax Cuts — Shame about the Spending", Backgrounder (Toronto: C.D. Howe Institute).

Robson, W., J. Mintz and F. Poschmann (2000), *Budgeting for Growth: Promoting Prosperity with Smart Fiscal Policy,* Commentary No. 134 (Toronto: C.D. Howe Institute).

HOW DO RECENT TAX REFORMS AFFECT THE BEHAVIOUR AND WELFARE OF FAMILIES?

Michael Smart, University of Toronto

Introduction

This paper reviews a number of reforms in personal income taxation enacted in the 2000 budget and discusses in particular their implications for the economic decisions of Canadian families. Evidently, estimating the behavioural impacts of tax reforms is a crucial step in assessing their implications for the excess burden of the tax system, for the level of economic activity, and ultimately for the welfare of Canadians. Unfortunately, reliable quantitative evidence on the effects of taxes on economic behaviour in Canada is quite limited. In what follows, I review the basic principles that should govern the design of the tax system, I discuss empirical evidence where available, and I attempt to identify areas where more research is needed. I first discuss the system of family benefits delivered through the tax system. Because these benefits are now targeted largely to low-income families, they impose very high marginal tax rates on some families, which has recently prompted concern among some economists. I then analyze two aspects of the retirement saving system that have been affected by recent reforms.

Marginal Tax Rates and Family Benefits

In the 2000 budget, the government expanded on recent reforms in the structure of the Canada Child Tax Benefit (CTB) system. The latest reforms announced are:

- An increase in the base CTB payment and also in the National Child Benefit Supplement (NCBS). The base payment will rise by $70 per child in July 2000. The NCBS, targeted at low-income families, will rise by $200 per child (relative to the levels announced in the 1999 budget). After the reforms, the maximum benefit will be $2,245 for the first child (compared to $1,805 prior to the 1999 budget) and $2,045 for additional children. Moreover, all CTB benefits are to be indexed to consumer price index (CPI) inflation effective January 2000. The government also announced its intention to raise the maximum benefit for the first child to $2,400 by the end of the five-year planning period.

- The NCBS will continue to be clawed back from recipients with net family income above $21,596. As a consequence of the increase in maximum benefits, therefore, clawback rates will rise. Beginning in July 2001, the new rates will be 12.9% for a family with one child, 23.6% for a family with two children, and 33.4% for a family with three children. (The corresponding rates announced in the 1999 budget were 11.5, 20.1 and 27.5%.)

- The income threshold at which the NCBS is fully exhausted and clawback of the base CTB payment begins is to be set equal to the middle bracket threshold, currently $30,004 but scheduled to rise to $35,000 by 2004. If all changes in the CTB are implemented as announced, therefore, marginal tax rates will ultimately decline for families in the NCBS clawback range, but more families will be affected by clawbacks.

- A reduction in the clawback rates for the base CTB is apparently also contemplated, to 2.07% for a family with one child, in place of the current 5% rate. A timetable for implementing this reform has yet to be announced.

The changes in the current budget therefore move further in the direction embarked on when the National Child Benefit system was introduced in 1997. Apparently, these reforms are an attempt to integrate the CTB with provincial social assistance and, in the process, dismantle the "welfare wall" that creates work disincentives for poor families with children. While the policies may well be having such salutary effects, it is important to ask whether they may at the same time be bringing the problems of traditional welfare programs into the tax system and, increasingly, subjecting the average Canadian family to the perverse incentives that were once reserved for welfare recipients. Poschmann and Richards (2000) argue forcefully that this is the case. They analyze the clawbacks associated with various federal and provincial family benefit programs and show that marginal tax rates typically range from 50 to 70% (and are, in some cases, even higher), even for moderately high family incomes.

As marginal tax rates have risen through the 1990s, economists have focused increasing attention on measuring their levels and debating their effects on economic activity. Davies and Zhang (1996) analyze the changes in marginal tax rate (MTR) schedules through the postwar period. They stress the long upward trend in the average of marginal tax rates faced by all taxpayers since 1949, but particularly in the 1960s and 1970s. Davies (1999) extends the analysis to address recent tax reforms and provides a useful review of economic principles that can guide the design of an income tax system and the evaluation of existing MTR schedules. High MTRs are unambiguously undesirable, as they create disincentives to work and pay taxes. Moreover, high MTRs do not per se increase progressivity in the tax system. However, high MTRs for some taxpayers are a necessary condition for a progressive income tax system that targets tax relief to those that need it most. If the tax system is to apply low or negative *average* tax rates to low-income families but high average tax rates to those with higher incomes, it follows that some taxpayers with intermediate incomes will face high *marginal* tax rates.

While these principles are unlikely to be controversial, they are perhaps not particularly useful either. As a practical matter, the difficult question is where in the income distribution those high MTRs should be levied. Economists argue that there are three basic principles that should govern this choice. First, a high MTR is proportionally worse the more people there are in the relevant tax bracket. Second, a high MTR is proportionally worse the higher the wage rate received by taxpayers in the relevant bracket. This second principle often seems to be overlooked in the debate about welfare and the working poor. It simply reflects the fact that work disincentives are more costly to the economy as the labour that is being lost becomes more valuable. Stated baldly, this principle implies we should spend more time worrying about tax disincentives faced by stockbrokers than by high school dropouts. Third, a high MTR is more costly when applied to a tax base that is more responsive to tax rates; when, for example, affected taxpayers may easily substitute from paid work to unpaid family care, or from conventional employment to activities in the less-taxed informal sector, and so on.

As high clawback rates for family benefits begin to affect taxpayers at two-thirds of median family income, each of these principles tells us we should look seriously at disincentive effects induced by the CTB. But if clawbacks are indeed driving MTRs too high, two very different directions of reform might be contemplated. First, the clawback rates might be reduced, mitigating the disincentive effects and spreading them over a greater number of taxpayers.[1] Alternatively (and somewhat paradoxically) clawback rates could be increased, which would concentrate disincentive effects on a narrower income band and therefore affect fewer taxpayers.

It is interesting to note that economists writing on the subject in Canada appear quite evenly divided on this issue. Economists at the C.D. Howe Institute in particular have recently called for reductions in clawback rates (Robson, Mintz and Poschmann, 2000). At the same time, others have expressed caution about this tendency for the clawbacks to creep their way up the income distribution (see, e.g., Boadway, 1999; Davies, 1999). After reviewing this debate, a reader is apt to be left with few definitive conclusions. For some, however, there are compelling reasons to believe that targeting of family benefits should be maintained and perhaps even enhanced, so that redistribution can be achieved while MTRs are confined to the places in the income distribution where they can do the least harm. But the focus of the recent debate on marginal tax rates misses some important complexities in the analysis of disincentive effects. A high MTR discourages an individual from working additional hours (and may have other effects as well, such as

---

[1]This strategy is implicit in the government's decision to raise the break-even threshold for the NCBS to $35,000, which will reduce MTRs for an affected family with two children by about eight percentage points.

on work in the informal or underground economy, self-employment and so on). But the decision of whether to participate in the labour force, and the choice between full-time and part-time work, depends more on the difference in average tax rates between low and middle income levels than on the MTRs levied at specific points in the distribution. A policy that clawed back more benefits from low and middle income families might have very undesirable effects on participation, particularly of secondary earners. This is especially true now that the federal Working Income Supplement has been abolished.

This suggests that planners must evaluate the trade-off between hours disincentives and participation disincentives in designing the tax system. Which effect is more important is fundamentally an empirical matter. Unfortunately, there is very little evidence for Canada that might inform the current debate. In particular, the literature provides no hard evidence about the effects of the reforms of the 1990s on the labour supply patterns of affected families in Canada. *Faute de mieux*, policy analysts in Canada must rely for the present on research into the effects of similar programs in the United States to assess the impact of family tax benefits. The U.S. Earned Income Tax Credit (EITC) in fact closely resembles Canada's CTB, albeit with some important differences discussed below. In 1996, the maximum benefit was about C$5,500, phased in with a subsidy rate of 40% of adjusted gross income (AGI), and then clawed back at a 21% rate on AGIs between $17,000 and $26,000. The clawback can lead to total MTRs in excess of 50%, high by U.S. standards but well below the tax rates currently induced by the corresponding Canadian programs.

Eissa and Liebman (1996) examined the effects of a small increase in EITC — the maximum benefit rose about $400 in 1987. Their approach relies on the idea that the policy change should affect single women with children (who were eligible for EITC), but not single women without children. On the other hand, these two groups should be affected in about the same ways on average by changing labour market conditions, or whatever else was changing over the reform period. That is, the 1987 reform can be regarded as a rough "experiment" to determine the impact of taxes on single mothers, where single women without children serve as a control group for other factors, unrelated to the reform, that affect the behaviour of all. Eissa and Liebman found substantial effects on participation by single mothers: their participation rate rose 2.8 percentage points relative to that of single women without children. At the same time, there was no discernible drop in hours worked by women already in the labour force, despite the disincentives associated with the clawback and the income effects of the transfer. More recently, Meyer and Rosenbaum (2000) found even greater increases in participation by single mothers (relative to the appropriate control groups) following the much larger reforms in incentives during the 1990s. They also report some evidence that participation increased more in states that have adopted their own supplementary EITCs. This observation affords us greater confidence that the observed changes in behaviour are indeed the result of the tax changes, and are not merely due to the surging U.S. economy of the 1990s.

Naturally, one should be careful in applying these results to Canada. (For a more extensive review of this literature and its implications for Canada, see Mendelson, 1997.) For example, labour supply of women is often estimated to be more responsive to after-tax wage rates in the United States than in Canada. As well, the U.S. policy is directed at single mothers, and married women with children might respond very differently to the Canadian policy. (For example, the clawbacks might influence their choice between full-time and part-time work.) Nevertheless, there is evidence that participation responds to tax incentives more than do hours. It follows that the high MTRs in the current system may be less important than the effects that would result from a badly designed targeting system. Certainly, as provincial governments reform their own earned-income supplements, following the introduction of the National Child Benefit system and the abolition of the federal Working Income Supplement, it is an opportune time to look for concrete evidence about the costs and benefits of this strategy.

Marginal Tax Rates and Efficient Taxation: Some Methodological Notes

A central message from this area of research is that tax rates do matter in individual economic decisions, so that policymakers would do well to think about the implications of reforms for MTR schedules and hence for the behaviour and economic welfare of taxpayers. The recent interest of a number of Canadian economists in calculating marginal tax rate schedules is a useful step in this direction. It tells us how various tax provisions interact, and it is a starting point for analyzing behavioural impacts. As well, the concept of the *average* marginal tax rate, advanced by Davies and Zhang, gives a useful though necessarily approximate indication of the overall disincentives in the tax system.

Nevertheless, the existing methodology has its limitations. First, as I have argued, the impact of MTRs on individual behaviour vary substantially, and the magnitude of these effects is an empirical matter. Consequently, high MTRs are not always associated with large efficiency costs. This suggests that a great deal more empirical research is required before policy analysts draw strong inferences about the economic consequences of various tax provisions, such as the CTB. Second, it is now common to use graphs of marginal tax schedules (as functions of taxable income) to gauge the effects of the tax system. This can be deceptive. Marginal tax rate schedules, particularly for families with children, exhibit "spikes" where various tax provisions interact, driving MTRs to high levels over narrow income bands. These spikes are surprising, and perhaps they offend one's aesthetic sense. But they probably have little effect on decision-making. Third, the average MTR, reported by Davies and Zhang (1996) and others, is a useful tool in tax policy analysis, but our goal should not be to minimize it. For technical reasons, the average MTR probably underestimates the true distortionary effects of taxes. As well, as I have argued, the effect of taxation on discrete economic decisions, like participation in the labour force or the informal sector, cannot be captured by marginal tax rate schedules alone.

Taxation of Retirement Incomes

Similar issues arise when one considers clawbacks in the various seniors' benefits (which were not addressed in the latest budget). These also lead to very high MTRs for low- and middle-income taxpayers. In this case, however, I consider disincentives to saving rather than to work. These disincentives seem to be especially strong for saving in Registered Retirement Savings Plans (RRSPs) and employer-provided Registered Pension Plans (RPPs). Since these plans shift taxable income to the retirement period, taxpayers in the clawback ranges are severely disadvantaged in making RRSP contributions. For many of them, they may even be better off saving in taxable form instead, or at least making withdrawals before retirement age. This is not only inequitable, it may go some way in explaining the low take-up rates for RRSPs among low-income taxpayers (Shillington, 1999).

It would be a mistake to exaggerate the magnitude of such effects. It is unlikely that many taxpayers with moderate incomes attempt to forecast future marginal tax rates before planning their retirement. Moreover, any who engage in such sophisticated tax planning will presumably also recognize that clawbacks can be avoided by withdrawing RRSP balances in the last few years before retirement.[2] Nevertheless, there is some support for this view. In recent research, Milligan (2000) has examined contribution patterns and shown that future marginal tax rates can have significant negative effects on contribution levels of individual taxpayers. So there is evidence that Canadians with retirement accounts do engage in forward-looking tax planning, and future policy reforms should be undertaken in light of this.

This raises a set of concerns too broad to be addressed here. Nevertheless, it is important to stress that the current system of clawbacks has, in the name of greater progressivity, created a situation that is horizontally inequitable for low-income Canadians who wish to save for retirement, and may have reduced the rate of saving as well. Shillington (1999) points out that the disincentives to retirement saving under the current system could be eliminated with the introduction of an alternative retirement savings vehicle in which initial contributions are not tax-deductible, but accruals and withdrawals after retirement are exempt from taxation.[3] This alternative vehicle preserves the tax exemption on accrued income that is the hallmark of our current system of RRSPs and RPPs, but it removes the uncertainty about future tax rates from the contribution decision.

---

[2]There is no penalty for withdrawals at any age, and early withdrawals are becoming increasingly common in Canada. This strategy allows taxpayers to avoid adverse tax consequences as long as their balances are not too large.

[3]A plan of this kind has recently been introduced in the United States as the Roth Individual Retirement Account.

Foreign Content Restrictions for Retirement Saving

The most recent budget affected one aspect of the retirement savings decision by increasing the foreign content limit that applies to assets in RRSPs and RPPs. It was announced in the budget that the limit is to be increased over the next two years to 30% from the current 20%.

What is this reform likely to be worth to Canadians? The real cost of the limit is related to the fact that returns to a broad portfolio of Canadian assets are not strongly correlated with returns to foreign portfolios. Consequently, investors and pension plans which diversify internationally obtain a form of insurance for uncertain retirement incomes. International diversification allows investors to reduce the risk of their total portfolio, and so to hold more high-risk, high-return assets, both at home and offshore. Our current policy of restricting foreign content therefore tends to increase risk and reduce average levels of retirement incomes.

A number of researchers have tried recently to estimate the gains from diversification that would result from a relaxation of the limit. The most common approach is to form a hypothesis about how investors would change their mix of domestic and foreign stocks and bonds following an increase in the foreign content limit, based on standard asset allocation models. But this approach may be problematic, given that standard models of asset allocation do not explain well the portfolio decisions of typical investors. In particular, there is far too much debt and too much domestic content in most retirement portfolios to be consistent with the theory. Consequently, it is somewhat heroic to predict how portfolios would change following a reform in the foreign content limit.

In a recent paper, Kevin Milligan and I (2000) have taken a different approach to this question. We examine the reform in the early 1990s, which raised the limit from 10% to the current 20%, and estimate its impact on average returns on actual portfolios that were held by investors. Our research exploits the fact that publicly traded mutual funds that identify themselves as RRSP-eligible are also constrained by the limit, whereas RRSP-ineligible mutual funds are not. Since the foreign property restriction is the only apparent difference in the two classes of funds, the impact of the policy can be estimated by examining how risk-adjusted returns of eligible and ineligible funds changed following the previous reform. We studied a large sample of equity funds in Canada, controlling for differences in market risk across the two kinds of funds, and for the observed performance of a broad index of Canadian stocks.

According to our estimates, the 10% increase in the limit of the early 1990s increased risk-adjusted returns to constrained portfolios by about 15 to 30 basis points per annum. While our approach is not fully comparable to previous methodologies, our estimate appears broadly similar to, but somewhat larger than, the findings of other researchers. In our view, the estimated cost of the policy is quite substantial. To place our estimates in perspective, I observe that the book value of stocks held in RRSPs and RPPs currently exceeds $450 billion. According to our estimates, increasing the foreign property limit to 30% is predicted to increase annual returns to these assets by as much as $1.4 billion annually.[4]

Based on standard excess burden calculations, few other tax reform measures could generate an efficiency gain of comparable magnitude. Thus, while the foreign content reform receives relatively little attention from the media and policy analysts, it might be regarded as the "sleeper hit" of the latest budget. Of course, there remains the possibility that foreign content restrictions produce other benefits for Canadians, which may be lost with the reform. It is sometimes suggested, for example, that the policy makes additional funds available for domestic investment and reduces the cost of capital for Canadian firms. While this view may have had some validity when the current policy was enacted in 1971, with the increasing integration of global capital markets in recent years, these effects have largely been attenuated. Canada currently maintains no international capital controls other than the pension foreign property limit. Since Canada is small relative to the world market, the domestic cost of capital is largely determined by world market conditions, rather than domestic supply and demand. It follows that the additional capital that is retained in the domestic market as a consequence of the foreign property rule merely displaces foreign investment funds, with

---

[4]This is in fact a conservative estimate, since the market value of pension equities substantially exceeds their book value, and the calculation ignores the increased return to future retirement saving.

no impact on the cost of capital or the aggregate supply of capital. Moreover, the impact of the policy on Canada's balance of payments is likely to be small, as many domestic investors can move non-pension wealth offshore to counteract the effect of the policy. These arguments notwithstanding, the foreign property rule might be held to serve other public policy objectives important to Canadians. If that is the case, it is important to recognize that these objectives have been achieved at a substantial cost to pension plan beneficiaries.

References

Boadway, R. (1999), "Retain Targeting, But Make Credits Refundable", *Policy Options* 20, 18-19.

Davies, J. (1998), *Marginal Tax Rates in Canada: High and Getting Higher*, Commentary No. 108 (Toronto: C.D. Howe Institute).

__________ (1999), "Control Spending to Cut Both Taxes and Tax-Backs", *Policy Options* 20, 20-21.

Davies, J. and J. Zhang (1996), "Measuring Marginal Income Tax Rates for Individuals in Canada: Averages and Distributions Over Time", *Canadian Journal of Economics* 29, 959-975.

Eissa, N. and J. Liebman (1996), "Labour Supply Response to the Earned Income Tax Credit", *Quarterly Journal of Economics* 111, 605-637.

Mendelson, M. (1997), "The WIS that Was: Replacing the Canadian Working Income Supplement", Discussion Paper (Ottawa: Caledon Institute of Social Policy).

Meyer, B. and D. Rosenbaum (2000), "Making Single Mothers Work: Recent Tax and Welfare Policy and its Effects", NBER Working Paper No. 7491 (Cambridge, MA: National Bureau of Economic Research).

Milligan, K. (2000), "How Do Contribution Limits Affect Contributions to Tax-Preferred Savings Accounts?", Discussion Paper (Toronto: University of Toronto).

Milligan, K. and M. Smart (2000), "What's the Cost of the Foreign Property Limit in Canada's Pension Rules?" *Policy Options* 21, 36-40.

Poschmann, F. and J. Richards (2000), *How to Lower Taxes and Improve Social Policy*, Commentary No. 136 (Toronto: C.D. Howe Institute).

Robson, W., J. Mintz and F. Poschmann (2000), *Budgeting for Growth: Promoting Prosperity with Smart Fiscal Policy*, Commentary No. 134 (Toronto: C.D. Howe Institute).

Shillington, R. (1999), *The Dark Side of Targetting: Retirement Saving for Low-Income Canadians*, Commentary No. 130 (Toronto: C.D. Howe Institute).

TAX CHANGES IN THE 2000 FEDERAL BUDGET

Robin Boadway, Queen's University

Much attention has been paid to the reductions in tax rates in the budget, and more generally on the division of the potential surplus into tax cuts, expenditure increases and debt reduction. I would like to focus more on tax reform aspects. Many of the structural changes in tax policy were incremental changes in the existing tax system, and in themselves were not too exceptional. Nonetheless, from the point of view of tax reform, they do raise a number of issues of principle. In most cases, the rationales for the structural changes in the tax system were not spelled out very carefully in the budget documentation. There is therefore a need to expose them to the scrutiny of the underlying principles of good taxation design.

I shall focus my comments on a small number of main areas. These include three specific measures: the capital gains exemption, the reduction in corporate tax rates and the Child Tax Benefit. As well, I shall briefly discuss what I regard as two overriding issues of general and ongoing concern: refundability in the income tax system and the allocation of tax room between the federal and provincial governments.

The Capital Gains Exemption

The capital gains exemption was increased with little or no explicit justification. In order to evaluate this measure, it is worth considering the rationale for the exemption in the first place. One can discern three possible rationales in the literature. The traditional one is to compensate for the absence of indexation of capital income in a rough and ready way. Capital income does remain unindexed, but the rates of inflation that we are now living under presumably do not warrant a one-third exemption of capital gains from taxation. Moreover, the benefits of deferring taxation until realization could more than offset the absence of indexation.

A second argument seems to be based on the notion that risk-taking and innovation will be encouraged, although the mechanism is not often made explicit. The theoretical literature on taxation and risk-taking is at best agnostic on this issue. Indeed, the thrust of the traditional literature is that taxation on the returns to risky assets should actually increase private risk-taking. Perhaps the concern is more with the effect of the capital gains tax on keeping risk-takers and innovators in the country, although this seems a very expensive way of accomplishing that objective.

The third rationale for the capital gains exemption is that it acts as a means of integrating the personal and corporate taxes. This was the view taken by the Mintz Committee, and it seems to be the most persuasive argument (although it would certainly not explain the preferential capital gains treatment in the United States where there is otherwise no integration).

Taking the integration rationale as being the reasonable one, several critical comments can be made. Most important, the capital gains exemption is a very poor device for integration. Unlike with the dividend tax credit, it does not distinguish between capital gains on domestic corporations versus capital gains from all other sources, which should not be integrated. Also, the exemption method implies that the degree of integration rises with incomes. Apart from that, there is the issue of the appropriate rate of capital gains exemption for integration purposes. The Mintz Committee argued that the three-quarters exemption effectively put capital gains and dividends on a par for persons in the top income bracket. If that is the case, increasing the exemption would put capital gains at an advantage relative to dividends. Apart from being unfair, this would provide an incentive to firms who use internal financing. These are not the firms that one would typically want to help.

From a tax design point of view, there seems no reason not to treat capital gains and dividends on a par. This would involve taxing capital gains fully, but having a capital gains tax credit available on capital gains earned from Canadian corporations. The rate of credit would be exactly the same as for the dividend tax credit, and the gross-up and credit method would be used to calculate it.

Corporate Tax Reductions: A Panacea?

The Mintz Committee did a very thorough review of the business tax system. They made a number of recommendations, one of which was to reduce the corporate tax significantly. This seems to have been the only aspect of the rate-reduction base-broadening thrust of the Mintz Report that has been taken up. Is it enough?

The advantages of a corporate tax cut by itself should not be underestimated. It reduces the incentive for firms to locate elsewhere. It also reduces the erosion of the tax bases through international profit shifting (e.g., transfer pricing, reallocating debt, etc.). And, it reduces in a modest way the differential tax treatment of different industries.

But, general corporate tax reductions go only part way to the objective of creating a level playing field among different investments in Canada. Differential treatment of different industries and investments remain very much in place. Moreover, there are some real disadvantages to a rate reduction in itself. It favours those corporations that are in a taxpaying position, but does nothing for loss corporations. Arguably the most serious problem with the existing tax system is its discriminatory treatment of losses, given that loss corporations are among those involved in innovative, risky and investment-intensive activities. A rate reduction also helps old and new capital indiscriminately, implying that a good deal of "costless" revenue might be forgone. Unfortunately, this seems difficult to avoid.

This is not to argue that corporate tax rate reductions were not well founded. The case seems pretty clear that they are necessary. The more general question of what is the correct corporate tax rate remains a tricky one. International comparisons can be a bit misleading. For example, the fact that the United States has a classical system while Canada partially integrates the personal and corporate taxes makes direct comparisons between statutory rates in Canada and the United States of limited use.

In the long run, corporate tax rate reductions are not sufficient. The case for removing the existing discriminatory treatment of various industries is a strong one. Moreover, it is one that would have been much more easy to accomplish politically when rates are being reduced rather than in a revenue-neutral setting when there are bound to be losers.

Canada Child Tax Benefit (CCTB)

The CCTB was both enhanced and extended to families with higher incomes. This is a gradual movement in the direction of a more universal system of child support, one that seems to be favoured by a number of interest groups and economists. The issue of the tax treatment of children is a highly vexing one. It involves not just matters of tax equity but also social values on which reasonable persons may differ. What follows is one observer's overview of the issues and conclusions about desired directions of reform.

There are various possible arguments for the special treatment of children in the tax system. First, children add to the number of persons in a household who must share the family's total income. More children entail less consumption for the remaining members of the family and therefore lower real income per person. Second, a more forceful version of the first point, and one that various recent commentators have focused on, is that the cost of raising children is a non-discretionary expenditure for parents and ought to be treated as other non-discretionary expenditures. The standard view on non-discretionary expenditures owes much to the Carter Report, which argued that non-discretionary expenditures ought not to be included in the tax base. (They would have argued for a deduction for non-discretionary expenditures, while many people have taken to arguing for a credit.) Third, the opportunities afforded children in their future lives vary according to their family circumstances. The principle of equality of opportunity along perhaps with social insurance notions suggests that society ought to have some responsibility for ensuring that children have comparable opportunities. Indeed, the ideal of equality of opportunity is now enshrined in our constitution. This argument would suggest targeting support to children in disadvantaged families. Fourth, in at least some societies (not excluding some parts of Canada), support for children is justified as a means of encouraging fertility, and this might support universality of benefits. Finally, there are those who would argue that the family as a social institution ought to be encouraged to flourish.

Depending on which of the above arguments one accepts, one will opt for varying degrees of targeting versus universality in the CCTB system. The most serious argument that has been put for universality concerns the idea that the costs of raising children are non-discretionary. (I am discounting the argument in favour of encouraging fertility; others may choose not to.) I would argue that this non-discretionary cost argument is tenuous for a number of reasons. The main argument against it is to challenge the idea itself. Having children for most persons is fully voluntary (and tax collectors could not sort out those for whom it is not). Moreover, the expenditures devoted to raising children are utility enhancing: they make parents happy. On those grounds, it is not clear why the costs of raising children should be treated any differently than the costs of housing, eating, etc. On top of this, society already puts enormous resources into children, such as education, health, libraries and recreational facilities. Child-care expenses are deductible for working parents. For stay-at-home parents they are not. But stay-at-home parents obtain the imputed income associated with household production at no cost. But, perhaps the biggest argument for tightly targeting child support is the equality of opportunity one. To the extent that equality of opportunity is taken to be a serious objective of government, those whose opportunities are clearly the most prejudiced are children in poor families. This suggests to me that the social value of money spent on children is still much higher at low-income levels than it is elsewhere.

There is, of course, the legitimate concern that targeting transfers to low-income families implicitly introduced high marginal tax rates on income. And, those tax rates will be higher the more targeted are the transfers. This is an issue quite separate in nature from the argument for universality, and should not in itself be used as the basis for demanding universality. It is an inevitable consequence of targeting that marginal tax rates are increased. Indeed, it is a persistent finding in the optimal income tax literature that marginal tax rates decline with income. What is really at issue is the trade-off between efficiency and equity.

My conclusion with respect to the CCTB is that it should remain a highly targeted program and not be extended into the upper reaches of the income distribution. The opportunity cost of extending the CCTB is in my view very high. It seems to me that the funds that were used for this purpose could better have been used to target transfers to the poor people with no children. They were the real (and maybe only) losers in this budget.

General Issue I: Refundability

I now turn to two issues of enormous importance that ought to be on the tax reform agenda, or at least subject to debate, in the near future. The first of these is refundability, whose absence in the income tax system is in my view its single most serious flaw. It is an issue that is relevant for both the personal and the corporate tax systems. Consider these in turn.

One of the major innovations in the personal income tax was the advent of refundable tax credits. These are now well established as means by which the federal government can deliver social policies through the income tax system. They are obviously relevant for the debate on targeting versus universality. Indeed, there might not be much of a debate if it were not possible to target transfers through the tax system.

Given this ability of the federal tax system to make credits refundable, an obvious question is: Why should there be any non-refundable tax credits? There seems to be no logical reason why the principle of refundability should not be extended to all tax credits. On the contrary, the case is very strong for doing so. Persons in a non-taxpaying position are treated abysmally by the federal tax system. They receive paltry sums under the existing refundable tax credits. The absence of refundability of all tax credits effectively leaves the poorest members of society at the mercy of provincial welfare systems, where they do not fare particularly well and where the incentives to earn can be heavily blunted. To re-emphasize a point made earlier, the only group not to gain much from the budget were the poorest off households without children. It is hard to think of a good reason why personal tax credits should not be refundable.

The arguments for refundability in the case of the corporate tax are quite different. The absence of refundability of business tax losses constitutes one of the most serious sources of differential tax treatment in the system. Loss firms tend to include growing, risky firms, many of which are small and are involved in large investments. These are also often firms for whom the costs of finance are relatively high. (Large firms have the ability to offset losses in one area of operation against profits elsewhere, and they have better access to internal financing.) And the problem is exacerbated by the growing use of profit-insensitive taxes documented by the Mintz Committee. Refundability would not only remove the discriminatory treatment inherent in the tax system, it would also assist with the financing of small, new firms.

General Issue II: Federal-Provincial Tax-Room Sharing

An issue very special to the Canadian context, and one that is rarely subject to policy scrutiny, is the appropriate sharing of tax room between the federal and provincial governments. Over the past few decades, the share of the income tax room has gradually but inexorably moved in favour of the provinces. This has occurred iteratively as part of the gradual process whereby the provinces have been required to assume greater and greater responsibility for raising their own revenues. There is a lot at stake here, and the issue is important enough to at least be subject to public debate.

Two issues in particular arise in this connection. On the one hand, as the provinces become more and more important in raising their own revenues, the strains on the system of tax harmonization become more and more telling. The income tax system is becoming more and more fragmented. We are now seeing the latest consequences of this as the provinces quickly move to a tax on income system. This development, which was foreseen long ago, is really based more on inevitability than on desirability. It has the potential of leading to forms of tax competition among provinces that are destructive from the perspective of an efficient and equitable internal economic union. It seems highly unlikely that the very effective system of income tax harmonization that was developed over a period of time can be sustained. Those who promised that decentralization would herald a new era of cooperative decision-making to replace what was seen as federal unilateralism may have their views put to a severe test.

The flip side of the turning over of tax room to the provinces is that the leverage the federal government has via its transfers to the provinces is becoming seriously diluted. This leverage seems to me to be a necessity if the federal government is to participate in a meaningful way in the coming debates over social policies for which they share with the provinces constitutional responsibility. The acrimony that has arisen over the federal government's share of provincial health expenditures, and the feeble response that tax points turned over almost 25 years ago still constitute part of the federal contribution, may well be a harbinger of things to come.

Session Four
THE EXPENDITURE DIMENSION

FEDERAL EXPENDITURES IN CANADA: The Millennial Vision and its Tensions

Lars Osberg, Dalhousie University

The Budget Plan tabled in the House of Commons on February 28, 2000 begins with the assertion that it "sets out the federal government's plan for Canada in the 21st century". To this end, it projects expenditure and revenue to 2003 and establishes a long-term rule for the level of federal expenditures. Of course, there may be some level of cynicism that such a long-term plan will be the victim of the priorities of the next federal re-election campaign — but this paper takes the budget at its face value. (One reason for doing so is the budget's early announcement of future tax cuts, and its indexation of the income tax system, which builds in a constraint on future expenditure initiatives.)

This paper argues that an enduring long-term vision must be both politically and economically sustainable, and the paper's major theme is a discordance between the level and allocation of rhetorical and financial emphasis that runs through the budget speech. This discordance is produced by, and is evidence of, a gulf between popular preferences and elite opinion that poses a real problem for the long-term sustainability of current federal financial planning.

I would like to thank Lynn Lethbridge for her exemplary work on this project and the Social Sciences and Humanities Research Council of Canada for its financial support under Grant 010-97-0802.

Other papers in this volume speak to the tax side of the federal accounts, but in analyzing the expenditure side, it seems natural to consider first the total level of spending and then the allocation of expenditure among competing alternatives. Since a federal government budget is both a political and an economic document, this paper considers the level and allocation of both rhetorical and financial expenditure.[1] Underlying this approach is the hypothesis that if a plan for the twenty-first century is to endure, it will be helpful if there is some consistency between its rhetorical and actual emphases.

In the hierarchy of "big issues" of political economy, surely one of the biggest issues is the relative size of government — and the budget speech has big news. It notes that "federal government spending, as percentage of GDP, is at its lowest level in 50 years ... program spending next year will be 4 billion dollars lower than it was when (the Liberals) took office in 1993" (Canada, 2000a, p. 8). The budget document continues: "Let there be no doubt — we will control spending ... growth in program spending is projected to be in line with inflation, plus population growth". This commitment to freeze government spending in real per capita terms implies that as per capita real GDP grows, federal government expenditure will continue to shrink as a percentage of Canada's economy.

The importance of this announcement of a small and forever declining role for the federal government in Canadian economic and social life is hard to overstate. It means that the cuts to federal expenditures that have marked the last seven years are not to be seen as temporary belt tightening. Although Canadians were encouraged to think of expenditure restraint in terms of the necessary sacrifices needed to solve a deficit problem, Canada's federal budget is now in surplus, but there is no intention to restore expenditure. This announcement is thus highly important, indeed historic. Surely if this was thought to be a politically popular initiative, one would have thought that the message of "reducing the size of government" would have been repeated throughout the budget document. Instead, it is mentioned only briefly on page 8 (taking up approximately 1.2% of the total length of the

---

[1]The measure of rhetorical discordance proposed here is the variance of the "PURC" (Per Unit Rhetoric Cost, billions of dollars spent per page allocated in the minister's budget speech).

budget speech). Although the introduction and the conclusion are full of rhetoric on the brighter future and better lives that await Canadians, the long-term trend in the size of government receives no explicit mention in either.

The importance of the issue raises the question: *Why* is this trend to a smaller federal government downplayed?

It should not be thought that reducing the size of the federal government has been a small achievement. As Figure 1 indicates, total federal program spending fluctuated in the range of 15% to 16.2% from 1959-60 to 1989-90 but is forecast at 11.6% in 2000-01. In fact, from 1951 to 1994, total federal spending was only once below 14% of gross domestic product (GDP).[2] In 1948-49 total federal program spending (including transfers to the provinces) was 10.3% of GDP and in 1949-50 it was 11.5%.[3] In sum, since World War II, there are only two years in which federal spending fell short of the 11.6% of GDP which is anticipated for 2000-01, and since federal spending will not in future reflect real per capita growth, future years will have an even lower federal share of GDP.

However, the 1948 to 1950 period was exceptional. 1940-47 was dominated by the war effort, when federal expenditure was a considerably higher fraction of aggregate national output. Hence, the federal government budget documents understate the level of achievement of program expenditure control. One really has to go back to the 1930s to find a similar span of time in which federal government expenditure has been a comparable share of aggregate Canadian GDP.

An even stronger, and in many senses truer, picture is obtained if one nets out transfers to the provinces, and looks at what the federal government itself does. Federal expenditures on goods and services and direct transfers to individuals will be 9.3% in 2000-01, a considerable decline from 12.2% in 1989-90 or 12.9% in 1959-60 (and one-tenth less than the 10.3% of 1949-50). Hence, if the issue is direct contact with citizens, either through

---

[2]In 1965-66, at 13.7% of GDP.

[3]All figures from Fiscal Reference Tables, are available at http:/www.fin.gc.ca/afr/frt99e.pdf

Figure 1: Federal Spending as a Percentage of GDP in Canada

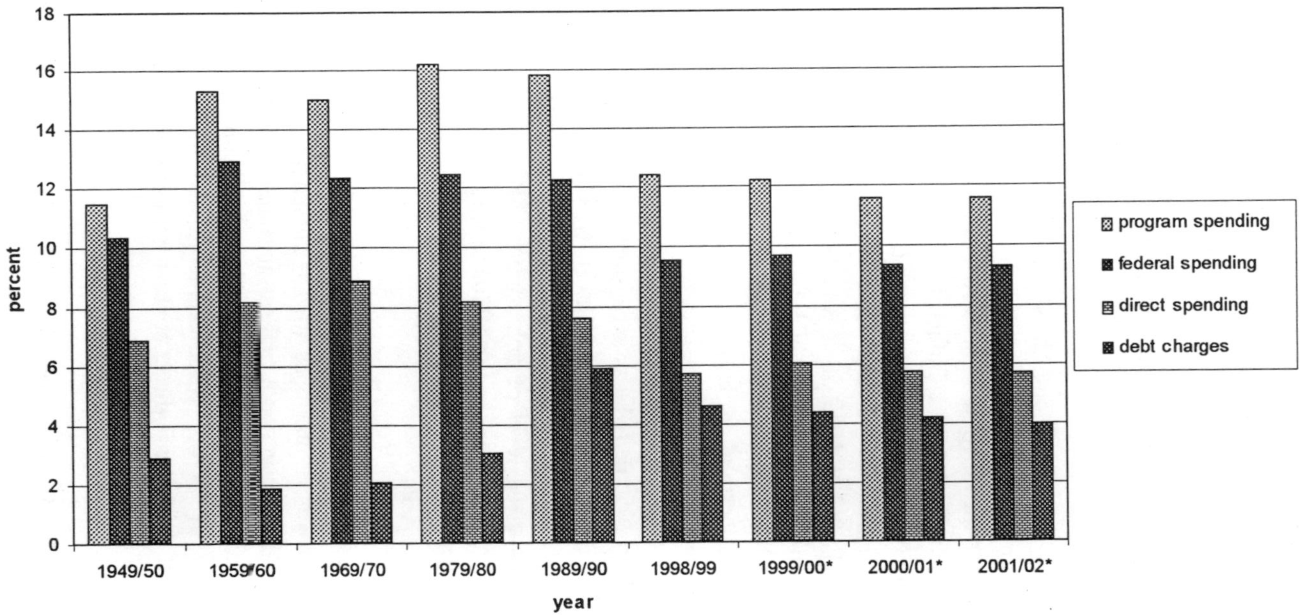

Notes: * Projected.
Federal spending = program spending — transfers to provinces.
Direct program spending = federal spending — transfers to individuals.

Source: Canada (2000a,b,c); Perry (1989).

services or transfers provided, the federal government is clearly at a 60-year low.

Figure 2 shows federal and provincial program expenditures as a percentage of GDP to make the point that although direct federal expenditure on goods and services and transfers to individuals were fairly constant as a percentage of GDP for the best part of 40 years, provincial government expenditures have grown significantly. Although in 1949-50 direct federal spending dwarfed provincial government spending (10.3% compared to 5.8% of GDP), by 1969-70 the provinces and the federal government were close to a balance and by 1989-90, federal expenditures were only about 70% of provincial government spending (12.2% compared to 17.1%). For the last quarter of the twentieth century, the federal government was, in expenditure terms, the "junior order of government", and the disparity in size has increased with time.

Figure 3 illustrates the fact that the federal government in Canada is significantly smaller, as a fraction of GDP, than the federal government in the United States. Whether measured in terms of total expenditures, or program expenditures (i.e., excluding debt charges) or direct spending (i.e., excluding transfers to other levels of government), the federal government in Canada spends significantly less, as a fraction of GDP, than the federal government in the United States. The difference cannot be explained by defence spending (which has fallen significantly in the United States as a fraction of GDP). The projections of the U.S. and Canadian budgets imply that in 2002, non-defence federal government program spending in the United States will be 12.8% of GDP, approximately one-sixth higher than the corresponding percentage in Canada.[4]

It may take some time before stereotypes of a large and overbearing federal government waste away, but in a remarkably short period of time, Canadians have gotten a smaller federal government. Whether considered as a fraction of aggregate GDP compared to previous decades, or relative to the expenditure of provincial governments, or relative to the expenditure of the

---

[4]For U.S. data, see United States (2000, p. 49, Table 3.1); for Canadian data, see Canada (2000b, p. 66, Table 3.6).

Figure 2: Federal and Provincial Program Expenditures as a Percentage of GDP

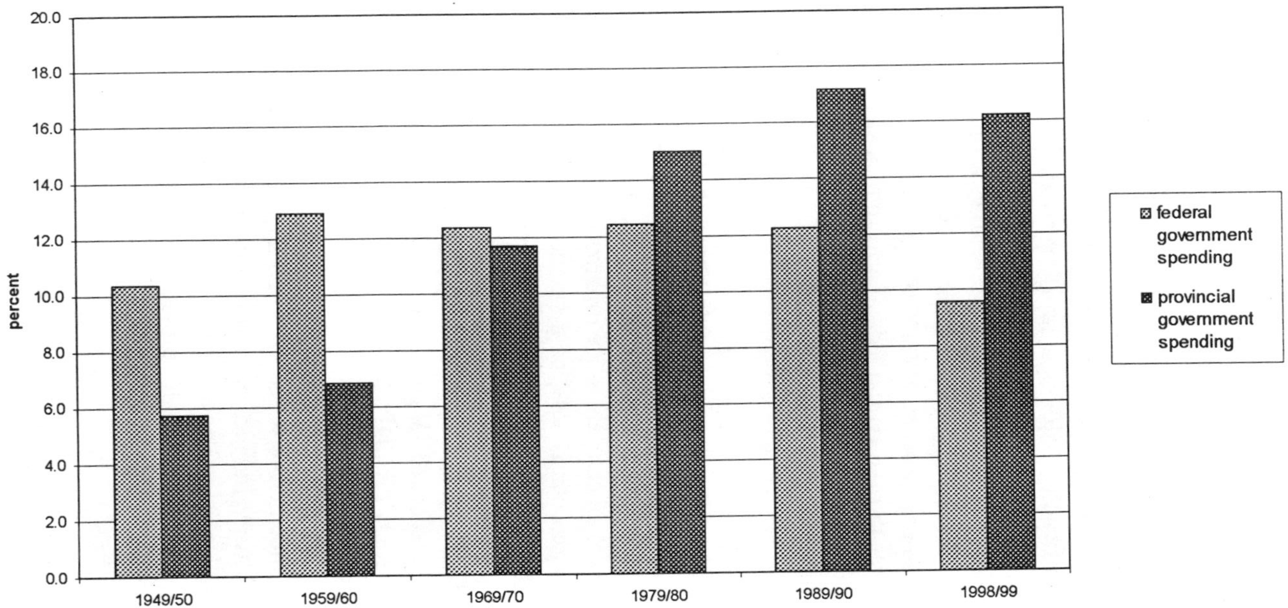

Note: Figures exclude debt charges. Transfers to other governments are excluded from the federal figures.
Source: Canada (2000a,b,c); Perry (1989).

Figure 3: Federal Government as Percentage of GDP Canada and the United States 1999-2000

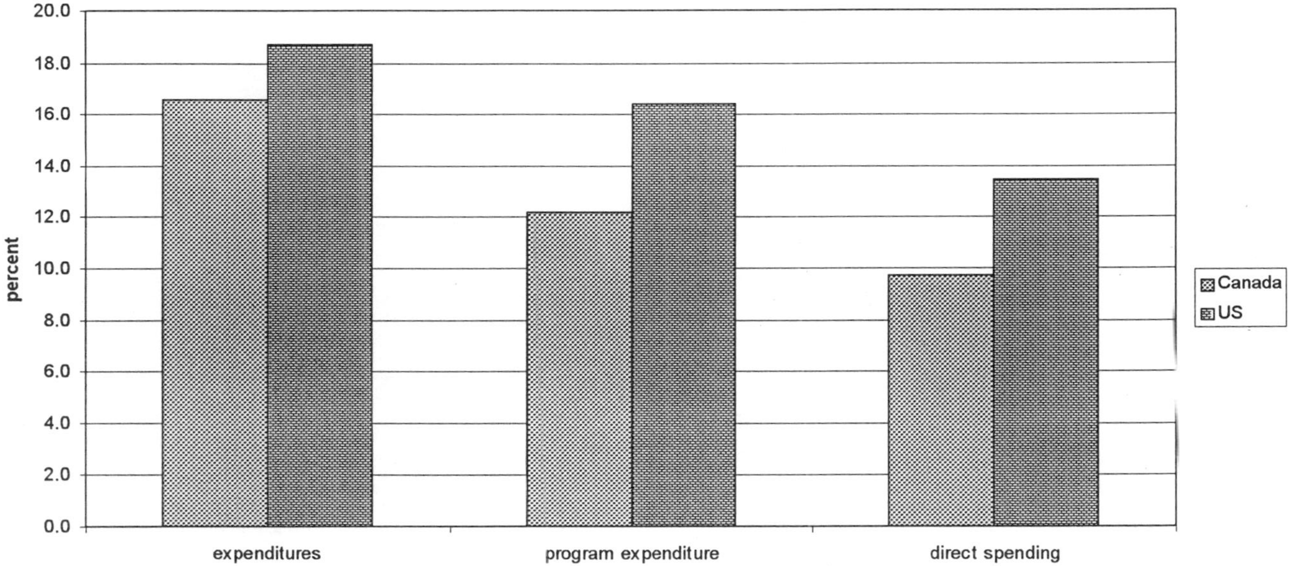

Notes: Program spending = total expenditure — debt charges.
Direct spending = program spending — transfers to other levels of government.

Source: Canada (2000c); United States (2000).

United States federal government, the government of Canada is now smaller and is forecast to get smaller still.

Canadians may be getting a smaller federal government, but is there any evidence that this is what they want? Figure 4 reproduces an Ekos poll of 1999 which indicates that American and Canadian attitudes to federal government budget planning are fundamentally similar. The wording of the question is a forced choice, in which respondents are prevented by design from saying that they want both more spending and lower taxes. A majority of both Canadians and Americans prefer increased expenditure on social programs like health and education to the alternative of either reducing the debt or cutting personal income taxes. Other polling results are quite comparable. Canadians regularly rank health-care spending, education, child poverty, crime and justice, environmental degradation, improving economic productivity and unemployment above such issues as reducing the national debt or cutting the level of taxation (Ekos, 1999). Only in 1994, and only for a brief period of time, did the national debt jump into prominence above health care or unemployment as a public priority for the federal government.

In a 1997 Ekos poll, for example, between 90% and 93% of respondents stated that they wanted to see government increase or maintain its involvement in the areas of unemployment, job training, transportation safety, education, health care, job creation, environment and managing our natural resources. In every case but transportation safety, the split between those who wanted to "increase" or "maintain" government involvement was strongly for "increase" (61% to 30% for unemployment, 59% to 32% for job training, 65% to 25% for education, 65% to 28% for health care, 65% to 26% for job creation, 57% to 37% for environment and 54% to 39% for managing our natural resources). An increased or maintained government role was supported by somewhat fewer when the issue was promoting international trade (89%), social assistance (81%), promoting Canadian identity and culture (78%) or immigration (70%), but these are still substantial margins in favour of a more activist government (Ekos, 1997).[5]

---

[5]The percentage of respondents who express a preference for eliminating a government role is typically 1% to 2%, except for the cultural promotion question, which hits 7% (Ekos, 1997).

Figure 4: Preferred Budget Emphasis

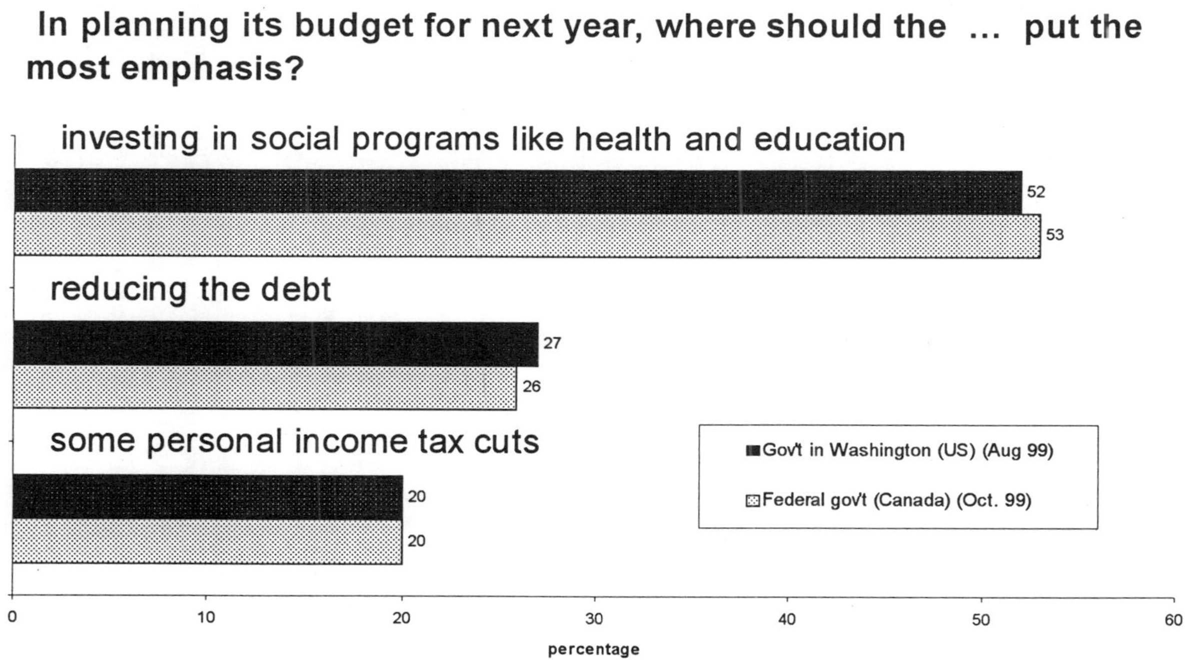

Source: Ekos Research Associates Inc. <URL: http://www.ekos.com/press/DEC22/sld008.htm>

Certainly there is no support in these numbers for a long-term shrinkage of the federal government's role in Canadian economic and social life.

Indeed, one way of reading the budget speech is as evidence that the finance minister knows that public attitudes favour greater spending to meet social problems. The minister's budget speech itself is 21.5 pages long, much of which (pages 9-17) is devoted to an extended discussion of spending initiatives, under the headings of the new economy, skills and knowledge, supporting research, the environment and children. Given the rhetorical emphasis devoted to these issues, one might have thought that there would be a corresponding cash expenditure. However, the total additional spending over the next five years under these initiatives amounts to a rather modest $2.9 billion, some 5% of the size of the tax changes simultaneously announced.

Table 1 itemizes the spending initiatives and tax changes discussed in the budget speech. Pages in the speech can be seen as an indicator of what government thinks the public wants to hear, while dollars of budget cost reflect actual choices made. Putting the political and the financial together, one can calculate the PURC of each initiative. The disparity in PURCs can thus be seen as an index of the mismatch between words and deeds in the federal budget.

Although the federal government announced increased health and post-secondary transfers of $2.5 billion (over four years) and municipal infrastructure spending of $2.1 billion, such transfers to other levels of government have limited rhetorical opportunities, and occupied in total less than a page of the budget speech (PURC = 5 and 5.25 respectively). Expenditures on high-tech initiatives such as research chairs, genome research, environmental technology and innovation centres received far more rhetoric (6.2 pages) but considerably less money. The PURC for research chairs was, for example, only 0.3 — less than a tenth the PURC for intergovernmental transfers. Cash transfers to encourage research reflect an activist approach to encouraging innovation, with the hope of long-term benefits to productivity, but the money involved was less than 2% of the cost of tax cuts. The really big money in the 2000 federal budget was the $58 billion in tax changes announced, whose cost per page (PURC = 9.66) dwarfed that of all federal spending initiatives.

Table 1: Words and Dollars: Initiatives Announced in Budget Speech

PURC[1]	*Total $B Cost*	*% of Tax Cuts*[2]		*Pages*
5.00	$2.5	4.31	Increase in health and post-secondary transfers	0.5
5.25	$2.1	3.62	Municipal infrastructure[3]	0.4
0.30	$0. 9	1.55	Research chairs[4]	3
1.80	$0. 9	1.55	Increase for CFI	0.5
0.32	$0.16	0.28	Genome research	0.5
0.32	$0.7	1.21	Environmental technology	2.2
0.34	$0.24	0.4	Farm aid	0.7
9.66	$58		Tax changes ("Relief")	6

Notes: [1] PURC = per unit rhetoric cost = (announced cost $billion) ÷ (pages in budget speech).
[2] Total spending over five years as % cumulative tax reduction ($58 billion - p. 22).
[3] $450M in first two years + three years @ $550M; health and post-secondary spread over four years; environmental technology spread over three years.
[4] "New economy" (pages 9, 10) hard to allocate - PURC for all research = 0.49.

Why is there such an extreme imbalance between rhetoric and reality in the federal government's budget documents?

Why does the minister of finance feel compelled to talk so much about some things (the spending initiatives) while actually doing so much more on the tax cut front?

Why is so much attention paid to spending initiatives (which are a small share of the operations of a federal government that is shrinking in relative size), while so little attention is paid to the aggregate size of the federal government?

If it really were the case that Canadians wanted a smaller role for the federal government in Canadian social and economic life, then one would expect a reverse sort of emphasis. When one sees in the budget document tables with headings like "Improving the Quality of Life for Canadians and their Children" and "Making Canada's Economy More Innovative", it is clear that the presentation of the budget document has been carefully calculated so as to maximize political popularity.[6] Hence, it is altogether likely that the federal government knows that most Canadians want their government to play an activist role in meeting pressing social problems, certainly that is what their pollsters are telling them.

My own opinion is that Canadians would be quite willing to accept a private sector solution to social problems, if that should happen. It seems to me that the number of Canadians who are ideologically in favour of increased government involvement on principle is small (and from the polling numbers, it is clear that the number who are *in general* against government involvement is *very* small). My opinion is that Canadians are fairly pragmatic, and that *if* the trend to a smaller federal government produces good results, then it would be accepted.

However, cuts to the welfare state have been going on for some time now, and as yet there is little sign of improved living standards. Although average incomes have recently begun to revive with the decline in the unemployment

---

[6]When asked "If you were Prime Minister for a day, and had to pick an overall national goal for Canada to achieve for the year 2010, which of the following would you choose?", respondents to an Ekos poll picked "best quality of life in the world" as their top priority followed by "best health care system", "lowest incidence of child poverty", and "lowest crime rate/safest community". The option "lowest overall tax burden" was 20 percentage points below "quality of life" at number 7. See <http://www.ekos.com/press/dec22/sld007.htm>

In earlier times, budget tables headings listed the ministry that was to be responsible for each spending initiative — information that was not presented in the February 2000 documents.

rate, the budget plan itself notes (Canada, 2000b, p. 28) that real per capita income in 1999 has not yet recovered the loss of the first half of the 1990s. In average real income terms, Canadians are still worse off now than they were in 1989. Throughout the decade the concentration of income gains at the top of the income distribution has meant especially little recovery in consumption for the bulk of the population.

Furthermore, one of the implications of cuts to social assistance and Unemployment Insurance has been an increase in poverty in Canada, (at the same time as poverty has been falling in the United States; see Osberg, 2000). Since living standards depend on the level of economic security with which individuals face the future and on the poverty and inequality that are produced by the distribution of total income, full calculation of trends in living standards shows a fall in recent years (Osberg and Sharpe, 1998). And Canadians continue to be concerned about the erosion of their "social wage" of public services, particularly health care.

If rapid and prolonged economic growth were to produce rising living standards throughout the income distribution, presumably many malcontents would be quieted. However, the prospect for such growth depends heavily on the demand management decisions of the Bank of Canada, whose sole priority remains maintaining very low inflation. As of the time of writing (May 2000) the Bank of Canada was demonstrating, yet again, its proclivity for strangling nascent growth by raising interest rates, even though the core inflation rate was only 1.3% (close to the bottom of the announced target range), and declining.

The more likely prognosis for the Canadian economy, therefore, is slow to moderate growth and a continuation of the chronic excess capacity that has characterized the Canadian labour market in the 1990s. It is possible that Canadian expectations are now so low that *any* growth in living standards will be interpreted as a welcome change, but one implication of "globalization" is the fact that citizens increasingly make international comparisons. Since the U.S. Federal Reserve has successfully emphasized growth as a priority, and continues to do so, comparison with U.S. outcomes will continue to show what could have been achieved. It is therefore possible that most of the public will have good reason for dissatisfaction with economic outcomes. Future years are therefore likely to see continuing tensions between a public that wants an activist government, and a policy elite that wants a shrinking federal role.

References

Canada (2000a), *Better Finances, Better Lives: The Budget Speech 2000* (Ottawa: Department of Finance).

__________ (2000b), *Better Finances, Better Lives: The Budget Plan 2000* (Ottawa: Department of Finance).

__________ (2000c), Fiscal Reference Tables, available at <http:/www.fin.gc.ca/afr/frt99e.pdf>

Ekos Research Associates (1997), “Rethinking Government”, available at <http://www.ekos.com/rg971/97-1.htm>

__________ (1999), *Long Term Tracking of Priorities*”, available at <http://www.ekos.com/press/dec22/sld006.htm>

Osberg, L. (2000), “Poverty in Canada and the USA: Measurement, Trends and Implications”, Presidential Address to the Canadian Economics Association, Vancouver, June 3, 2000, forthcoming *Canadian Journal of Economics*.

Osberg, L. and A. Sharpe (1998), “An Index of Economic Well-Being for Canada”, Research Paper R-99-3E (Ottawa: Applied Research Branch, Human Resources Development Canada).

__________ (2000), “International Comparisons of Trends in Economic Well-Being” (with Andrew Sharpe), *American Economics Association*, January 7, 2000 (Boston, Massachusetts).

Perry, J.H. (1989), *A Fiscal History of Canada: The Post War Years*, Canadian Tax Paper No. 85 (Toronto: Canadian Tax Foundation).

United States (2000), *Budget*, Historical Tables, available at <http://w3.access.gpo.gov/usbudget/fy2001/pdf/hist.pdf>

FEDERAL BUDGET 2000: The Expenditure Dimension from a Provincial Perspective

Lise Bastarache, Royal Bank of Canada

In its latest budget, the federal government added a $2.5 billion supplement to the Canada Health and Social Transfer fund (CHST), bringing the total CHST cash transfer to $15.5 billion, up from $14.5 billion in fiscal 1999-2000. Although this is higher than the amount allocated in both fiscal 1997-98 and 1998-99, it remains well below pre-deficit fighting levels. The purpose of this paper is to examine the change in total federal cash transfer payments (CHST and Equalization) per capita over a ten-year period, and its impact on provincial revenue.

Federal Transfers to Provinces

The federal government provides transfer payments to provinces through two major programs:

- The Canada Health and Social Transfer (CHST), which supports provincial health care, postsecondary education and social assistance and social services.

- Equalization transfers, which provide less prosperous provinces with federal money to assist them in offering programs and services. This ensures that programs and services are of comparable quality across Canada.

The Canada Health and Social Transfer (CHST)

The CHST came into effect on April 1, 1996, replacing the Canada Assistance Plan (CAP) and Established Programs Financing (EPF), and was extended for a five-year period by legislation in 1999. The CHST takes the form of a cash transfer and a tax transfer (tax room given directly to the provinces since 1977), in roughly equal amounts. Since 1998, the CHST has a cash floor of $12.5 billion, and will be allocated on an equal per capita basis beginning in 2001-02.

Equalization Payments

Created in fiscal 1957-58, equalization payments are currently given to seven provinces: Newfoundland, Prince Edward Island, Nova Scotia, New Brunswick, Quebec, Manitoba and Saskatchewan. Equalization payments, which the provinces are free to spend as they wish, have not suffered any cuts as opposed to CHST payments. They are calculated according to a formula which sets out a standard revenue-raising capacity. This standard measures the fiscal capacity of the five "middle-income" provinces: Quebec, Ontario, Manitoba, Saskatchewan and British Columbia. The Equalization program was renewed in 1999 for a five-year period.

For fiscal 2000-01, the standard revenue-raising capacity was estimated at $5,679 per capita. Among the seven "have not" provinces, Newfoundland had the widest gap with the standard, while Saskatchewan had the lowest. When a qualifying province's fiscal capacity declines relative to the standard due to a slowdown in its economy, its equalization transfer automatically increases. Conversely, when its fiscal capacity increases relative to the standard due to stronger economic growth, its equalization transfers decline. Equalization payments, however, are subject to "ceiling" and "floor" provisions. In April 1999, new provisions were put in place for the 1999-

2000 to 2003-04 fiscal period, with a $10 billion ceiling for fiscal 1999-2000. For the four fiscal years after 1999-2000, the ceiling increases at the same rate as the gross domestic product (GDP). As for the new floor provisions, they have been simplified and now provide the same protection for all provinces, regardless of their fiscal capacity. Equalization payment reductions on a per capita basis cannot exceed 1.6% of the standard revenue-raising capacity per capita of the five "middle-income" provinces. This amounts to roughly $90 per capita for fiscal 2000-01, as the standard revenue-raising capacity was estimated at $5,679 per capita.

Federal Budget 2000

The 2000 federal budget added a $2.5 billion supplement to the CHST fund, which the provinces can freely use over the next four years and will be allocated on an equal per capita basis — bringing the total CHST cash transfer to $15.5 billion, up from $14.5 billion in fiscal 1999-2000. According to government estimates, the cash portion of the CHST transfer will remain at $15.5 billion throughout fiscal 2003-04. Although this is higher than the $12.5 billion allocated in both fiscal 1997-98 and 1998-99, it remains well below the $18.8 billion of fiscal 1993-94. Between fiscal 1993-94 to 2003-04, CHST cash transfer payments will have declined by $3.3 billion, while equalization payments will have increased by $2.6 billion, for a total shortfall of $700 million in the major cash transfer payments to provinces over the ten-year period (Figure 1).

CHST Cash Payments Cuts: The Fiscal 1993-94 to 1998-99 Period

Between fiscal 1993-94 and 1998-99, CHST cash payments declined by $6.3 million, a 33.5% reduction, while equalization payments increased by $1.5 million, leaving the total cash portion of major transfers to provinces down by $4.8 million, an 18% reduction. All the provinces ended up with lower per

Figure 1: Federal Cash Transfers to Provinces

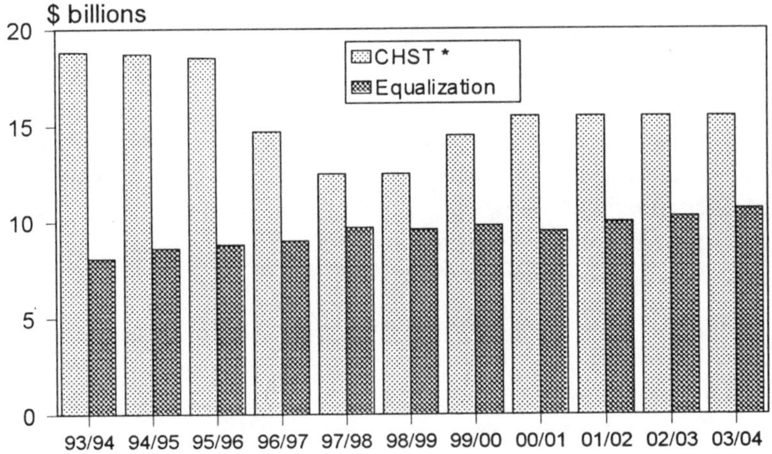

Note: *includes CHST payments to territories.
Source: Federal Budget 2000 documents.

capita CHST cash payments, but the hardest hit provinces in percentage terms were Ontario and Alberta. Among the provinces receiving equalization payments, Saskatchewan, Manitoba and Quebec suffered an overall federal transfer per capita loss, as their equalization payments were insufficient to cover the gap (in Saskatchewan, equalization payments per capita declined over this period, given an increase in the province's revenue-raising capacity). The Atlantic provinces were the only ones to enjoy a rise in their overall federal transfer per capita payments, as increased equalization more than offset the CHST cash payments decline (Figure 2).

Despite the 18% reduction in the total cash portion of major transfers to provinces over this period, total provincial revenue (own-source and federal transfers) per capita increased in all provinces. In percentage terms, the biggest gains occurred in Nova Scotia and Quebec, while the smallest increase was in British Columbia and Alberta (Figure 3).

Figure 2: Major Federal Cash Transfers to Provinces (CHST and Equalization)

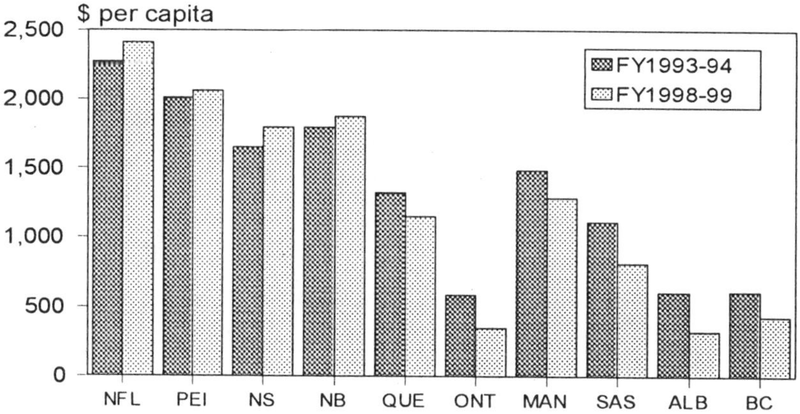

Source: Federal Government and Statistics Canada.

Figure 3: Provincial Revenue per Capita — Own-Source Revenue and Federal Transfers

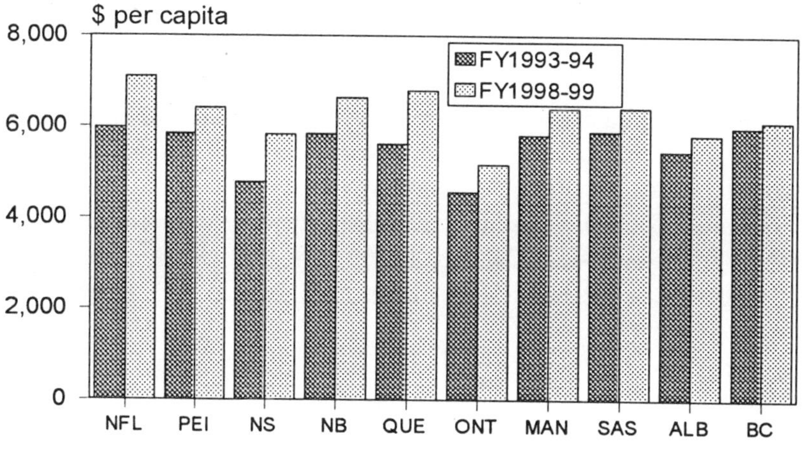

Source: Statistics Canada (FMS basis).

Provincial Revenue Simulations: The Fiscal 1999-2000 to 2003-04 Period

Beginning in fiscal 2001-02, CHST entitlements to provinces (cash and tax transfers) will be allocated on an equal per capita basis. Looking only at cash transfers, the specific amounts are $500 in fiscal 2001-02, $496 in fiscal 2002-03 and $492 in fiscal 2003-04. This means all provinces except Ontario and Alberta will see a decline in their per capita CHST cash payment (compared with fiscal 1999-2000), with Saskatchewan breaking even. However, most provinces are expected to have higher total cash payments (CHST and Equalization) in 2003-04 than in 1999-2000, as increased equalization payments per capita will more than offset the decline in CHST payments. Only in British Columbia and Saskatchewan are the numbers slightly lower in fiscal 2003-04 than in 1999-2000 (Figure 4). Looking at the longer ten-year period, total cash payments per capita in the Atlantic provinces are expected to be higher in 2003-04 than they were ten years earlier (fiscal 1993-94), while Manitoba remains at the same level (Figure 5).

Using the same assumptions on own-source revenue growth as in a previous study,[1] combined with the estimates on federal transfers provided by the Department of Finance and population estimates provided by Statistics Canada, we have projected total provincial revenue (own-source and federal transfers) per capita over the 1999-2000 and 2003-04 period. Despite only modest gains in federal cash transfers, the average annual growth rate in total revenue per capita is expected to reach at least 2.5% for all provinces over this four-year period, meaning that constant real per capita spending is not an unattainable goal (Figure 6). Furthermore, the provinces are expected to gain greater control and flexibility over their own source revenues beginning in the 2001 taxation year (January 1, 2001), as they will have the option of adopting a tax-on-income system for personal income tax (currently, only

---

[1]*Relative Fiscal Power: Ottawa versus the Provinces*, Royal Bank, September 1999.

Figure 4: Major Federal Cash Transfers to Provinces (CHST and Equalization)

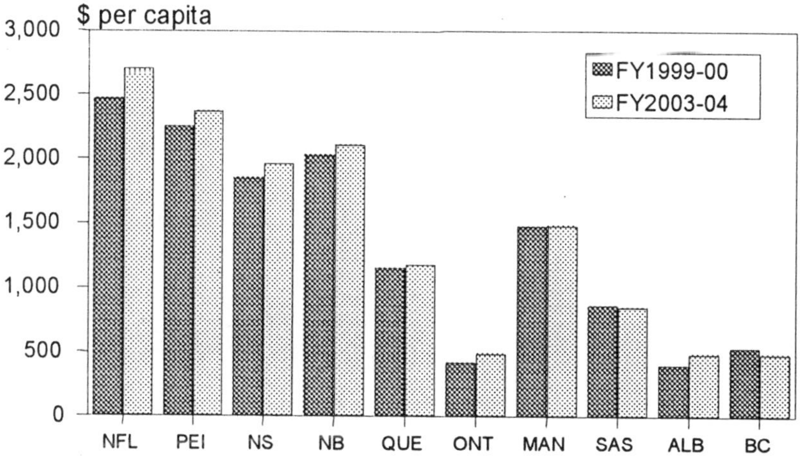

Source: Federal Government and Statistics Canada.

Figure 5: Major Federal Cash Transfers to Provinces (CHST and Equalization)

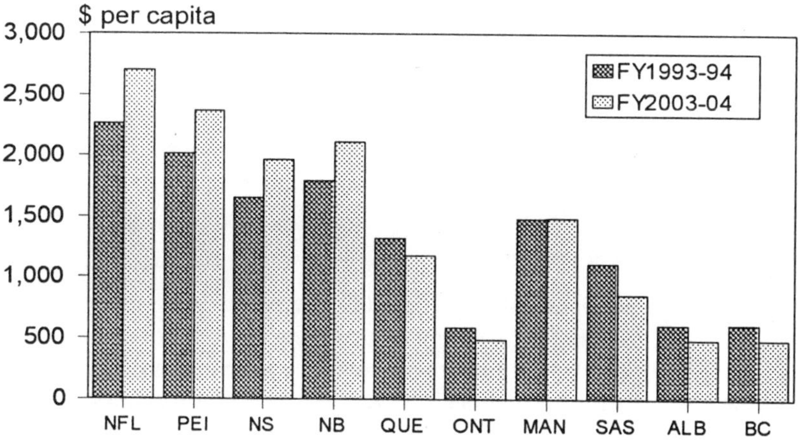

Source: Federal Government and Statistics Canada.

Figure 6: Provincial Revenue per Capita — Own-Source Revenue and Federal Transfers

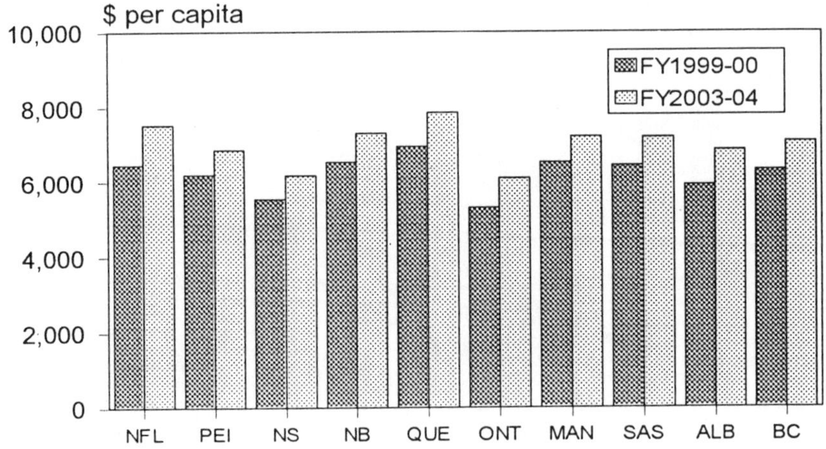

Source: Statistics Canada (FMS basis), Royal Bank Economics Department.

Quebec has such a system). Most provinces are expected to do so, and many have already made the announcement.[2]

Conclusion

From a provincial public finance perspective, the outlook for federal transfers/equalization payments is on a more solid footing now than during

---

[2]For the current taxation year (2000), the tax-on-tax system remains in place, but the provinces have the option of modifying payroll deductions (starting July 1, 2000) to offset federal income tax cuts. The federal government does not expect many provinces to "opt out"; if they wish to do so, they must make the announcement in their spring budget. As of writing this paper, only one province, Nova Scotia, had chosen this option, given its large expected deficit. As for the other provinces, the impact of the federal tax cuts on provincial revenue is expected to be modest in the current fiscal year.

the years of federal deficit reduction. With the prospect of continued balanced/surplus budgets at the federal level, massive cuts in provincial cash transfers such as those that occurred over the 1993-94 to 1998-99 period appear to be a thing of the past. Although cash transfers per capita have not returned to pre-deficit fighting levels, except in the Atlantic provinces, they should rise or remain relatively stable over the next few years in all provinces, as supplements have been added in the 1999 and 2000 budgets. Those supplements, however, are insufficient to halt the decline in the share of federal transfers to total provincial revenue, even in the Atlantic provinces. Under the assumption that the share of federal transfers continues to decline, the provinces will increasingly rely on own-source revenues to fund program spending, most of which will come under increasing pressure over the next decade (i.e., health and education). In light of this challenge, the move towards a tax-on-income system appears to be a prudent hedging strategy for the provinces.

Session Five
THE SOCIAL POLICY DIMENSION

BUDGET 2000: A Children's Budget?

Frances Woolley, Carleton University

The 2000 budget was initially rumoured to be a "children's budget". In the end, it was not. In this short paper I will outline the reasons why a children's budget was wanted and needed, what the budget actually provided in terms of support for families with children, and the broader implications of the budget in terms of Canadian social policy. I will argue that the budget was a missed opportunity. Funds were available to provide a more coherent treatment of families with children but, instead, child policy was confounded with a myriad of other goals.

Why a Children's Budget?

There were good reasons to anticipate that the 2000 budget would be a children's budget. Mounting concern about Canadian children's well-being had created pressure for action on child poverty. Children under 14 are more likely to experience low incomes, after taxes and transfers, than any other age group in Canada (Picot, Myles and Pyper, 1998; Phipps, 1999). Their vulnerability to poverty arises in part from the declining economic prospects

---

I would like to thank Andrée Houde, Alan MacNaughton and Carlos Del Castillo for careful comments on an earlier draft of this paper. However, the views expressed in this paper are my own and not those of the Department of Finance.

of their parents. Young men earned in 1994 the same, in real terms, as did their counterparts in 1969 (Corak, 1998). Family structure is another contributing factor. Thirteen percent of children under 14 live in single-parent families, and run an especially high risk of poverty (ibid.). Yet simply giving parents money is not an obvious solution to children's problems, since children whose parents receive government transfer income tend to have worse outcomes than those with employed parents (ibid.; Lefebvre and Merrigan, 1998).

Middle- and upper-income families were also pressuring for reforms to the tax treatment of families. Canada's main program for children, the Canada Child Tax Benefit, is targeted towards those with low and moderate incomes, and at present does not reach one out of five Canadian families. Canada's generous Child Care Expense Deduction cannot be used by families with an at-home parent, or for non-receipted child care, so is actually claimed by less than one-third of families with child-care expenses (Canada. House of Commons, 1999, p. 9). Parental leave under the Employment Insurance program is claimed for less than half of new births (Statistics Canada, 1999). The gaps in Canada's patchwork of programs mean that some families receive no recognition at all for their caregiving responsibilities (Vincent and Woolley, 2000).

In response to perceived inequities in Canada's tax treatment of families, the federal government created a Sub-committee on Tax Equity for Canadian Families with Dependent Children. The committee made a number of recommendations: expansion of the maternity and parental leave, a review of the Child Care Expense Deduction (CCED), allowing stay-at-home parents to contribute to pension plans and introducing a refundable tax credit available to parents who provide direct parental care (Canada. House of Commons, 1999). The 2000 budget only implemented one of these recommendations, expansion of maternity and parental leave, although a modest credit for stay-at-home parents of disabled children was also introduced. The CCED was unchanged by the budget, and no pension plan provisions were introduced.

Instead, the 2000 budget channelled funding for children into three key areas. The first initiative was expansion of the Canada Child Tax Benefit, with funding increases of $475 million in 2000-01 and $1,020 million the following year, with a cumulative total of $2.8 billion in increased funding by 2004.[1] The second initiative was a doubling of maternity and parental leave under the Employment Insurance program, projected to cost $900 million per year. Finally, families with children will benefit materially from the reductions to personal income taxes announced in the budget — reductions that will lower government revenues from personal income taxes by $2.8 billion in 2000-01, a further $4.6 billion the following year, with a cumulative impact of $13.3 billion by 2004. In the next part of this paper, I will evaluate each of these initiatives. Who are the key beneficiaries? How much do they benefit? What can we say about the broader economic impact of the programs?

Canada Child Tax Benefit

The Canada Child Tax Benefit makes a fascinating study in social policy. The tax benefit has two aims (National Child Benefit, 1999). The first is to promote parents' attachment to the labour market by removing the "welfare wall". Every time the federal government increases child benefits, provinces can, and generally do, reduce social assistance payments. As a result, parents receive more of their income from child benefits, which they can keep if they start working, and less from social assistance, which they lose if they start working. Incentives to go from welfare to work are thereby increased. At the same time, provinces have funds to reinvest in other programs that benefit children. The second aim of the Canada Child Tax Benefit is to reduce the extent of child poverty by providing greater benefits to low-income working parents. In 1996, the most recent year for which data are available, over half of low-income families had at least one parent working for at least part of the year.[2]

---

[1]CCTB figures are taken from Canada. Department of Finance (2000, p. 203), Employment Insurance cost estimates from Department of Finance (ibid., p. 139), personal income tax figures taken from Department of Finance (ibid., p. 156).

[2]National Child Benefit (1999), supplementary tables available on http://socialunion.gc.ca/NCB-99/a3c.html. A more detailed breakdown is: single-

The budget took a number of steps to enrich the child benefit. First, the CCTB will be fully indexed against inflation as of January 2000. Second, the child benefit supplement received by low-income families will be increased by $200 per child per year,[3] effective by July 1, 2001 (an increase of $170 for July 1, 2000, was announced in the 1999 budget). Third, the base benefit, received by all eligible families, has been increased by $70 per child, effective July 1, 2000. Of this increase, about $14 represents indexation due to inflation. Finally, the 2000 budget has raised the threshold at which child tax benefits are clawed back to $30,004, effective July 2000, up from the $29,590, the level announced in last year's budget for that date. The threshold will be further increased to $30,544, effective July 1, 2001. Both of these increases simply reflect indexation of the thresholds against inflation. By 2004, the government aims to increase the CCTB to $2,400 for the first child and $2,200 for the second child. By a combination of reduced tax-back rates and increased thresholds, the CCTB will be extended to nine of ten families with children.

Yet the most interesting aspects of the child benefit program are those not emphasized in the budget speech. Even with the changes, the CCTB will not mean much to some middle-income families. Although the total spending involved in these measures is substantial, the CCTB suffers from what could be called "the law of large programs". About 6 million children living in 3.2 million families receive child benefits (National Child Benefit, 1999). Every dollar increase in the base benefit amount costs $6 million and more, because higher benefit levels result in more families becoming eligible for benefits. Yet despite the large dollar sums involved, the increases in child benefits will only make a significant difference to low-income working families. For a working family with two children getting by on $20,000 a year, a $200 increase in the National Child Benefit supplement and a $70 increase in base benefits is worth $540, a 2.7% increase in income. For an average two-

---

parent families: 35.8% have some employment; two-parent families: 71.3% have some employment; overall: 51.3% have some employment.

[3]This $200 increase includes any increases due to inflation.

parent family, with an annual income (in 1997) of $60,721,[4] the $70 increase in base benefits announced in this year's budget amounts to about 0.1% of income, or 0.2% for a two-child family, an order of magnitude less significant.

There does seem to be an increasing awareness in Ottawa policy circles that some middle-income families are not well-served by Canada's present programs. One of the key points in the 2000 budget — the one that will contribute the most to extending CCTB coverage — is a plan to reduce the rates at which child benefits are taxed back as income increases. In 2004, the rate at which base benefits are taxed back as income increases will fall, from 5% to 4.14% for a family with two or more children, and from 2.5% to 2.07% for a family with one child. The plan to reduce tax-back rates is buried deeply in the budget documents (the new tax-back rates can be found in footnote 1, Table A7.13). Moreover, there is no firm commitment to reducing tax-back rates. This is unfortunate, since lower tax-back rates are the best way of guaranteeing that all families will receive some recognition of the cost of raising children.

It is also worth noting that the increases in child benefits will not help some of the poorest families in Canada. When the child benefit supplement for low-income families is increased, social assistance payments are reduced by an amount that varies from province to province. Since almost half of all low-income families, and 60% of single-parent families, receive some social assistance income,[5] the clawback of social assistance payments is a serious issue. Indeed, the child benefit supplement is not designed to help poor families on social assistance. It is designed to separate support for children out of social assistance, thereby removing the welfare wall, and at the same time provide funds to provincial social programs.

---

[4]Statistics Canada, http://www.statcan.ca/english/Pgdb/People/Families/famil22a.htm, May 29, 2000.

[5]National Child Benefit (1999), Supplementary Statistical Information, http://www.statcan.ca/english/Pgdb/People/Families/famil22a.htm. Actual figures are 60% of single-parent low-income families, 33% of dual-parent, low-income families and 46% of all low-income families received some social assistance during 1997.

Yet the child tax benefit moves the welfare wall, rather than removing it. Because the child tax benefit is targeted, at some point the money received in child tax benefits is taken away again. As the size of the benefit increases, so does the rate at which it is taxed back and/or the income range over which the tax-back applies. As of July 1, 2001, a family with two children, one under the age of seven, and an income of $21,596 receives $4,550 in child tax benefits. The same family with an income of $30,544 receives $2,440 in child tax benefits (Canada. Department of Finance, 2000). As a result, effective marginal tax rates increase by 23.6 percentage points for all two-child families with net incomes between $21,596 and $30,544. For a family with three or more children, the tax-back rate is even higher. When these tax-back rates are added to income taxes, Employment Insurance premiums and Canada Pension Plan premiums, the result is an effective marginal tax rate higher than that faced by some of Canada's top income earners. The replacement of social assistance with child benefits also raises questions of timeliness. Since child benefits are based on the previous year's income, will they be there when a family really needs them?

Given the problems with child poverty in Canada, it is hard to fault the federal government for trying to help poor families. The child benefit program is also laudable as a new model for federal-provincial cooperation (although Quebec has not participated in the NCB system, it has acted on its own in a comparable way). It would be very expensive to provide middle-class families — who after all make up the bulk of families in Canada — with enough benefits to make a difference. Much more political capital can be gained by providing large benefits to small groups of people. And child benefits do, in fact, reach many Canadian families. By way of contrast, the provisions for extended parental leave, the second major budget initiative, provide much larger benefits to a much smaller group of people.

Parental Leave

Increased parental leave provisions provide extremely generous benefits to a select group of families with children. The 2000 budget increases parental leave available through the Employment Insurance program from 10 to 35 weeks. The total amount of child-related leave available is doubled from six months to one year. The budget documents estimate that the program will cost $900 million and benefit 150,000 families. To put these numbers into perspective, in any given year the program will benefit fewer than 4% of Canadian families with children and less than half of all families with newborns. However the *increased* benefits per recipient family are projected to average $6,000 each.

If anything, the Department of Finance estimates of the per family benefits are conservative. Throughout the 1990s, maternity and parental benefits have averaged about $7,000 per beneficiary, with benefit levels for 1998 averaging $6,780 (Statistics Canada, 1999). At present the average claim, 24.5 weeks, is very close to the maximum claim allowed, 25 weeks. Given the high cost of child care and other employment related expenses, to say nothing of the pleasure of getting to know one's children, it seems reasonable to expect that most claimants will continue to take close to the maximum available benefits. If so, the increase in claims would be closer to $7,000 per beneficiary, for a total cost of over $1 billion.

The increase in parental leave provisions has been widely praised as an initiative that is good for children and parents. Yet there are awkward questions which are rarely asked or answered. First, less than half of births — 48.7% (Statistics Canada, 1999) in 1998 — result in a claim for benefits. The benefits under the new program will be so generous — an average benefit of close to $14,000 — one has to ask very seriously: Who is eligible? Who is excluded? Almost nothing is known about those not covered by Employment Insurance. Are they self-employed? If so, given the growth in self-employment over the 1990s, perhaps there is a case for a voluntary parental leave program for the self-employed. How many are excluded because of falling under the required number of hours? If it is a substantial number, the plan, announced in the budget, to reduce the number of hours of work required to claim benefits from 700 to 600 hours will produce a welcome expansion of benefits.

A second question raised by the maternity and parental leave program is this: if it is beneficial for parents to stay home with children — so beneficial that working parents receive close to $14,000 per year to do so — why are policymakers so anxious to get parents off welfare and into the workforce? There is a fundamental inconsistency between the philosophy underlying the

National Child Benefit, children are better off when their parents are working, and that underlying parental leave provisions, children are better off when parents are at home, at least for the first year of life.

Yet perhaps we should not look for philosophical consistency, but for political realities. The Employment Insurance program tends to be used disproportionately by seasonal workers, the low-skilled, those living in depressed regions and, because men are heavily represented in industries such as construction, fishing and forestry, by males. Maternity and parental leave is sometimes the only concrete benefit middle-class Canadians see from the Employment Insurance program. As such, it plays a crucial role in maintaining the program's political legitimacy. Maternity and parental leave has another political upside. It targets rather nicely a group that receives very few benefits from present Canadian child policies: dual-income families earning about $70,000 a year, those too affluent to receive much by way of child tax benefits but not affluent enough to benefit from the Child Care Expense Deduction.[6]

Tax Cuts

Maternity and parental leaves help middle-income, dual-earner families. Child benefits help low-income working families. But what about that $60,000 single-earner family, the family that was alleged to pay twice the tax

[6]The CCED is only worth using if the lower earner is in the middle or top tax bracket after child-care expenses and other deductions, otherwise the cost to the caregiver of declaring the income, paying tax, EI and CPP premiums, will exceed the tax savings from the CCED. A $70,000 family is unlikely to have the lower income earner in the middle or top tax bracket (see also Vincent and Woolley, 2000).

of a dual-earner family with the same total income,[7] the family that triggered so much of the concern about taxation and the family?

For "traditional middle-class" families, the most important budget provisions are the general tax relief. Reductions in personal income taxes will save a one-earner family of four $1,007 in 2001. In contrast, a dual-earner family with a 60:40 income split[8] and some child-care expenses will see their taxes reduced by $501 in 2001, less than half the tax cut experienced by the one-earner family.[9] Indeed, because so much of the funds available in the 2000 budget were directed towards general income tax relief, better-off one-earner families gained substantially from this budget.

Because the federal income tax is individually based and progressive, it inevitably treats dual- and single-earner couples differently. Dual-earner and single-earner couples only pay the same taxes under a flat-rate income tax schedule. This feature of flat-rate taxes is one of the key reasons for Alberta's proposal to adopt a flat tax. As reductions in federal taxes put pressure on federal-provincial tax collection agreements, other provinces, including Ontario, will move to a tax on base rather than a tax on tax, meaning that we can expect to see a widening variety of approaches to taxation and the family.

---

[7]A dual-income family making $30,000 (with each spouse earning the same amount and claiming maximum child-care deductions) would pay less than half the income tax owed by a single-income family making the same amount (i.e., $60,000) (Reform Party, 1999).

[8]That is, one person earning $36,000 and the other earning $24,000.

[9]These figures are taken from http://www.fin.gc.ca/newse00/data/00-051_2e.html.

Conclusions

Taking a broad view of the budget, we can see that it offered something for almost every family type: child tax benefits for low-income families, maternity and parental leave for middle-income, dual-earner families, tax breaks for better off single- and dual-income families. Yet what it did not offer was a coherent approach to family policy. This is unfortunate, because there are severe problems with the current Canadian policies towards families.

First, with a patchwork of programs, however generous, there is a danger that some people will not be covered. It is hard to come by information about the coverage and timeliness of child tax benefits and other programs, but the risk is real. Second, targeting benefits creates high marginal tax rates, especially in the $20,000 to $30,000 range. It can be argued that people's labour supply is not strongly affected by marginal tax rate and, indeed, economic evidence suggests the disincentive effects of high tax rates on labour supply is often overstated. More realistically, a family may find it advantageous to keep their net income for tax purposes at around $20,000 by combining legal work with work for cash, for example, running a home daycare, doing odd jobs, or working for tips in the service sector.

Third, as economists are beginning to know more about the connection between public policy and children's well-being, they are finding that not only do incomes matter, but the form of income matters. As noted above, children do better in families with higher levels of employment income, but not in families with high levels of welfare income. Shelley Phipps (1999, p. 123) provides a careful comparison of government policies and child outcomes, and argues that countries pursuing a more universal approach to policy have records "vastly superior" to those of countries that provide benefits only to poor children.

Canadians need to think seriously about how the costs of raising children are to be shared across society. Children are not like yachts, pure consumption goods that can be bought and sold at whim. They are future employees, taxpayers, nurses, accountants, caregivers of the aged. Keeping families healthy and sane now may be well worth the investment.

References

Canada. House of Commons (1999), *For the Benefit of Our Children: Improving Tax Fairness,* Nineteenth Report of the Standing Committee on Finance, Sub-Committee on Tax Equity for Canadian Families with Dependent Children.

_________. Department of Finance (2000), *Better Finances, Better Lives: The Budget Plan 2000* (Ottawa: Department of Finance Canada).

Corak, M. (1998), "Introduction", in M. Corak (ed.), *Labour Markets, Social Institutions, and the Future of Canada's Children*, Catalogue no. 89-553-XPB (Ottawa: Statistics Canada and Human Resources Development Canada).

Lefebvre, P. and P. Merrigan (1998), "Family Background, Family Income, Maternal Work and Child Development", <http://www.hrdc.gc.ca/arb/publications/research/w-98-12e.pdf>

National Child Benefit (1999), *National Child Benefit Progress Report: 1999* (Ottawa: Minister of Public Works and Government Services Canada). Also available at <http://socialunion.gc.ca>

Phipps, S. (1999), "Innis Lecture: Economics and the Well-Being of Canadian Children", *Canadian Journal of Economics* 32(5), 1135-1163.

Picot, G., J. Myles and W. Pyper (1998), "Markets, Families and Social Transfers: Trends in Low-Income among the Young and Old, 1973-95", in Corak (ed.), *Labour Markets, Social Institutions, and the Future of Canada's Children.*

Reform Party of Canada (1999), http://www.reform.ca/archive/families/family01.html#E10E4, March.

Statistics Canada (1999), "Employment Insurance Support to Families with Newborns", *The Daily*, October 25.

Vincent, C. and F. Woolley (2000), *Economics of the Household and the Taxation of Canadian Families* (Montreal: Institute for Research on Public Policy).

DO WE KNOW WHERE WE ARE GOING?

Keith Banting, Queen's University

> If you don't know where you are going, you may end up somewhere else.
>
> — Yogi Berra

Canadians are living through a period of transition, a period in which the country is moving from one grand policy strategy to another. Nowhere is this clearer than in the area of social policy. Over the last decade, program after program inherited from the postwar generation has been redesigned or restructured in response to new economic, social and political pressures. Because this transition is occurring through a long series of incremental steps, it is easy to miss its cumulative sweep. A partial view comes from the back of Budget 2000, where an impressively long list summarizes the changes introduced in the last three budgets. A comprehensive list of changes in federal budgets since the late 1980s would be daunting, and would have to be extended further to incorporate an equally pervasive series of steps at the provincial level. Virtually every component of social Canada has been reshaped in some way.

The incremental nature of this transition is hardly surprising. Indeed, it seems quintessentially Canadian. After all, the postwar welfare state was built in a similar fashion, one program at a time in a process that took over 30 years. Unlike the postwar period, however, the contemporary transition is taking place without the benefit of a comprehensive blueprint or vision to guide our incremental steps. There is no contemporary equivalent of the Beveridge Report or the Marsh Report, setting forth a broad understanding of the relation between economic and social policy and an integrated conception of diverse social programs. So the question naturally emerges: Do we know where we are going?

The question can be rephrased to ask whether the myriad of incremental changes at the federal and provincial levels are adding up to a model of social policy that is internally coherent and politically sustainable over time. The postwar model had such an internal logic. On one side, governments encouraged the progressive liberalization of the international economy through successive rounds of the General Agreement on Tariffs and Trade (GATT) and, in later stages, of their domestic economies through deregulation. On the other side, the expansion of social programs compensated for the risks inherent in economic liberalization. The formal purpose of postwar social programs was to provide security in an uncertain world through powerful income transfers designed to protect against the risk of poverty during unemployment, disability, illness and old age. But these programs also provided greater security from the shocks and economic turbulence inherent in a market economy in an opening world. In the words of one analyst, "governments asked their publics to embrace the change and dislocation that comes with liberalization in return for the promise of help in containing and socializing the adjustment costs" (Ruggie, 1994, pp. 4-5).

Fast forward to the contemporary debates. The outline of a new model does seem implicit in current policy debates in international organizations such as the Organization for Economic Cooperation and Development (OECD) and in domestic political forums. On one side, the model embraces a new wave of economic liberalization in response to globalization and the knowledge-based economy. On the other side, however, the model posits a change in the social role of the state. In contrast to the postwar approach to economic security, which sought to protect or cushion people from painful changes, the current approach holds that social policy should facilitate change and adjustment to the new economy. In this context, such security as is possible in the global era is seen to flow, not from income transfers, but from the skills and knowledge demanded by the new economy. The secret to success and economic security in the future, both for individuals and for countries, is therefore to be found in investment in education and training. At its heart, then, the new model is simple: embrace globalization and the knowledge-based economy, and adopt a conception of security rooted in human capital.

Two questions need to be asked about this model. First, are we actually adopting this approach in practice as well as rhetoric? Second, is such a model politically sustainable? A brief survey of policy trends in recent years suggests that the transition from discourse to practice is incomplete at best. We have clearly reduced the traditional instruments of social security through retrenchment in unemployment benefits and social assistance, and we have encouraged greater individual responsibility for building retirement savings through instruments such as Registered Retirement Savings Plans (RRSPs). These changes have represented a strategy of devolving and privatizing risk. The federal government has devolved greater responsibility for stabilizing incomes to provincial and local governments; and governments collectively have transferred more of the risk inherent in economic change to individuals themselves. The security index developed by Osberg and Sharpe (1998) gives one quantitative measurement of the extent of the erosion in the traditional instruments of economic security in recent years.

Despite these changes, it is not clear that we are actually adopting the approach to security celebrated in the new paradigm, enhanced investment in human capital. There have certainly been educational initiatives from both the federal and provincial governments. But it is hard to believe that, overall, Canada is strengthening its education and training systems and improving access to them. Recently, the Senate of Queen's University was in session, grappling with two items that reflect on this question. One was the difficult financial situation facing the university in light of the funding and tuition policies of the provincial government, the result of which has been yet another round of budget cuts for all academic units. As an academic administrator, I spent much of the 1990s making such cuts, and I was hoping that we were turning a page as we entered a new century. Apparently not. The second item on the Senate agenda was an impassioned plea by graduate and professional students about the impact of continuing tuition increases and the cumulative debt loads that they must carry. As I listened to those debates, I found it hard to believe that we are living in a country that is dedicated to a human capital strategy in practice as well as rhetoric.

It is also important to ask whether the contemporary policy strategy is politically sustainable. Will Canadians consider economic liberalization and an emphasis on human capital to be fair? Or will the fundamental legitimacy of the new paradigm be continually challenged? Answers to this question are inevitably speculative at this stage, but several observations seem relevant.

Building political legitimacy for the new paradigm will probably require two seemingly contradictory movements. Governments will have to take the paradigm seriously, and move beyond it. At one level, we need to take human capital seriously as a collective enterprise. The current policy trend is to transfer more of the cost of education and training to individuals and their families, privatizing the sources of security celebrated in the new social paradigm. The new strategy will not be legitimate or politically stable if access to education and training is not universal in practice as well as in theory. In my view, this will require a return to the language of social rights. The postwar generation established a *right* to security as they understood it. The logic of the new paradigm points to a comparable *right* to access to education and training. Establishing such a right in practice would represent a major change in direction for this country.

Taking human capital seriously, however, also requires going beyond the narrow bounds of education and training systems to confront wider barriers to achievement. Studies of the determinants of educational attainment make clear that social factors are powerful in shaping educational success. Societies with high levels of income inequality tend to have high levels of inequality in educational achievement. The causal relationships here are undoubtedly complex, running in both directions. But "the long arm of family" emerges strongly in this context. The social-economic status of parents, whether measured by their income or education levels, is critical to young people's educational achievements (see, for example, OECD and Statistics Canada, 2000). In addition, some minority groups perform less well in the educational sweepstakes and are not being equipped to soar in the new economy. Although the expansion of educational systems in the postwar era lowered structural barriers to education, we have not abolished the traditional adage that "birth is fortune". In this context, a retreat from wider social policy instruments that are critical to the well-being and development of children risks a retreat from access to the new economy.

Finally, building legitimacy for the new policy paradigm requires moving beyond its parameters in a wider sense as well. Even if the wider social determinants of educational inequality could be moderated and a radically meritocratic society established, the result might well be a more unequal society, with larger gaps between skilled knowledge workers on one side and their unskilled compatriots on the other. From this perspective, a human capital strategy alone might not be sufficient to sustain a sense of fairness and social cohesion. Canada and other industrial countries need to come to grips with the redistributive strategies essential as complements to a social contract premised on human capital. Otherwise, the exclusion of marginal groups and the creation of an underclass of low-skilled citizens may be the unintended consequence of the new social paradigm. Such an outcome would generate continuing political challenges — not only to the international trading system such as those mounted in Seattle and other cities, but also to the fundamental fairness of the domestic social contract.

Do we know where we are going? It is not at all clear that we have thought through the full implications of the policy paradigm that we have embraced in recent years. As a result, there is a danger that we will end up somewhere else.

References

OECD and Statistics Canada (2000), *Literacy in the Information Age: Final Report of the International Literacy Survey* (Paris and Ottawa: OECD and Minister of Industry).

Osberg, L. and A. Sharpe (1998), "An Index of Economic Well-being for Canada", paper presented at the CSLS Conference on the State of Living Standards and Quality of Life in Canada, Ottawa, October 30-31.

Ruggie, J. (1994), "Trade Protection and the Future of Welfare Capitalism", *Journal of International Affairs* 48, 1-12.

Session Six
ASSESSMENT AND PERSPECTIVES

PAUL MARTIN'S TAX REVOLT

Jim Stanford, Canadian Auto Workers

Whatever it was originally supposed to be called, Paul Martin's 2000 budget, perhaps his last, will undoubtedly go down in history as the "tax cut" budget. This was truly a watershed budget, probably even more so than in 1995 when he launched his hell-or-high-water assault on the deficit. Trying to reverse a 20-year legacy of chronic deficits and mounting debt was a challenge of daunting proportions. But five years later, with the deficit licked and fat surpluses looming, Martin's next task was even more fundamental: to map out a longer term vision of the role that Canadian governments will play in our society and our economy in the decades to come.

The response, coming from a Liberal administration, which still pretends to harbour dreams of ambitious social and economic interventions, was surprising. Governments, in the Paul Martin plan, will become still smaller. The programs they provide — including cherished ones like medicare and public education — will remain in a more-or-less permanent state of financial crisis, even as the economy around us becomes ever-wealthier. Canada's social and economic development will be guided even more by the pressures of unconstrained market forces than is already the case. Already well-off individuals will be allowed to keep even more of their private incomes, while income-support measures helping poor Canadians will become still weaker.

A different version of this article appeared in the April 2000 edition of *Policy Options*.

Martin's landmark tax cut budget deviated dramatically from the stated 50:50 formula on which the Liberals contested and won the 1997 election (50% of the surplus to social programs, the other 50% to tax cuts and debt reduction). Instead, this budget pledges to reduce taxes by at least $58 billion over the next five years. The true figure will probably be higher. Following tried-and-true practice, Martin's deliberately cautious timetable will allow future tax cuts to be implemented ahead of schedule, thus earning him another gold star for phony overachievement. He hinted strongly that the promised additional cuts to personal and corporate taxes will actually be implemented well before the 2004 deadline, a promise that is backed up by subsequent indications that the federal surplus for 2000 is running far ahead of plan. This could push the cumulative five-year value of the tax cut to $70 billion or even more.

The Finance Department currently estimates the latent federal surplus at just over $100 billion for those same five years. Martin, therefore, is allocating about 60% of that surplus to tax cuts alone, and probably more. Throw in $15-$25 billion for debt reduction (depending on how many of Martin's various contingency reserves are actually used for this purpose), and the 50:50 rule has suddenly become a 25:75 rule or even a 20:80 rule.

Political Math

This budget represents a gigantic step to the right by a federal government that still nominally claims to be committed to a more egalitarian and inclusive national vision. All the more curiously, Martin threw his eggs in the tax cut basket despite a bevy of indicators that the Canadian public was not especially interested.

Of course, if one only listened to business lobbyists and the minions of the Hollinger media empire, one would inevitably conclude that lower taxes are in fact the only issue of concern to Canadians. And indeed, when asked if they would prefer to have more money in their pockets, 99.9% of the public will answer in the affirmative. But when asked what is more important, tax cuts or a public health-care system that works, a powerful majority of

Canadians choose health care. And almost as many rank other priorities — especially public schools and postsecondary education — well above tax cuts in their shopping lists for how to spend the surplus. (See, for example, the results of an Angus Reid poll on this issue released February 6, 2000, or a similar Ekos survey from August 20, 1999.)

Most Canadians know that tax cuts are not free. Most understand the trade-offs implicit in the surplus-allocation exercise. If anything, the sense of public concern about the state of health care, education, and other essential services has grown. If the Liberals wanted to invest in health care and other public programs, they certainly had a public mandate to do so.

What political calculations led this government of purported egalitarians to side with the rich and powerful in this landmark budget? Perhaps the strategists saw more long-term political pressure from the right, including the new incarnation of the Reform Party, than from the left, and hence moved to undercut that pressure with a budget that is clearly the most conservative yet in a long line of conservative Liberal budgets. At any rate, the Liberals have clearly abandoned both the central platform of their election mandate, and the current desires of a clear majority of Canadians, with their aggressively one-sided roadmap for future fiscal policy. It will only be when the advocates of health care and education can impose a political cost on the government that equals or exceeds the pressure applied by business leaders, newspaper-owners, and the other partisans of tax rage, that we can ever expect a more balanced approach.

Of course, even tax cuts of these epic proportions could never be sufficient for the business lobbyists and other well-connected leaders of the tax revolt. While the business community, too, was surprised by the scale of Martin's tax cuts, its spin-doctors worked hard to contain their enthusiasm. After all, this is a game of goalposts. The business community could hardly come out and praise the government for its foresight, lest it be left with nothing further to demand next year.

An analyst from the C.D. Howe Institute defined the budget's tax cuts as "modest". An economist from Ernst & Young complained the tax cuts were "nickel and dime". The corporate tax reductions, under which statutory

Canadian corporate and capital taxes will fall to U.S. levels by 2004,[1] were decried as "piddly" by the Nesbitt Burns spokesperson. Advocates of social spending, meanwhile, could only sigh and hope that one day they might receive some "modest" new funding for health care, some "nickel and dime" support for higher education, and some "piddly" investment in a national child-care program.

How the War Was Won

The federal government will allocate the lion's share of future surpluses to tax reduction, even though it achieved the lion's share of deficit reduction as a result of reductions in program spending. Thus the "peace dividend" resulting from the successful war against the deficit is being handed out to those who did not really go to battle.

Figure 1 illustrates the disaggregation of the total improvement in the federal government's fiscal balance during the first five years of Liberal rule — from large deficit to small surplus. The contribution of each of the three major components of that favourable change are measured as shares of the gross domestic product (GDP). Business and tax-revolt leaders claim that the government taxed its way out of the deficit; this claim is simply false. Federal taxes rose only slightly as a share of GDP during Paul Martin's first five years as finance minister (by barely more than a point of GDP at their peak in 1997), and this increase accounted for only 15% of the shift in federal fortunes (again measured as a share of GDP) by 1999.

In fact, higher taxes were the *least* important factor behind the sharp turnaround in the federal balance. Reductions in program spending accounted for almost two-thirds of the improvement, while lower debt-service charges

---

[1]Effective Canadian corporate tax rates are already lower than U.S. levels thanks to generous deductions and rebates for depreciation, depletion and research and development. Including corporate tax reductions announced in the 2000 Ontario budget, even average statutory corporate tax rates will be significantly lower than in the United States within four years.

Figure 1: Sources of Federal Savings
(Deficit Reduction by Component, 1994-1999)

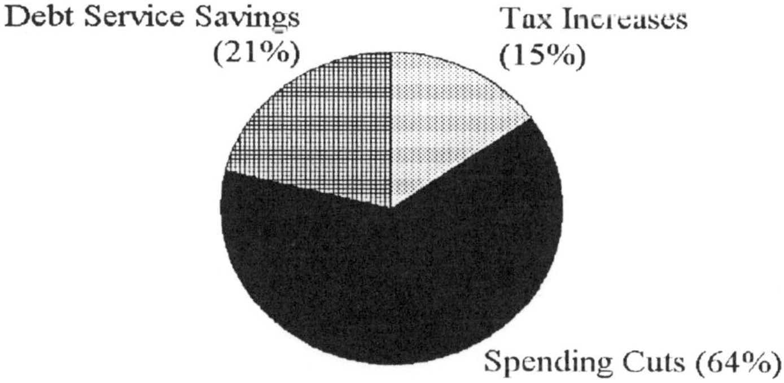

Decomposition of deficit reduction as share of GDP

(resulting both from a paydown of over $30 billion in market debt since 1996, and from a lower average effective interest rate paid on that debt) accounted for the remaining fifth.

Federal taxes have been falling relative to GDP since 1997. And now, with the firm two-year tax reductions announced in this budget, the modest post-1995 rise in federal taxes as a share of GDP will be fully reversed by fiscal 2001. By fiscal 2001, federal taxes will fall to the same level — just under 16% of GDP — as when the Liberals came into office (see Figure 2). In subsequent years, of course, that average tax rate will fall further, on the basis of Paul Martin's cautious tax cut timetable. On the tax side, then, the government has already more than fully unwound the fiscal "damage" incurred in the course of its mighty deficit-reduction effort.

The damage to federal program spending, however, is only getting worse. Program spending, of course, fell dramatically in the early years of the Liberal mandate, shrinking by fully one-fifth (measured as a share of GDP) between 1994 and 1996. The incredible thing, however, is that program spending has *continued* to decline, despite the attainment of balanced budgets, the generation of financial surpluses, and now the announcement of

Figure 2: Federal Taxes and Spending (1994-2001, % of GDP)

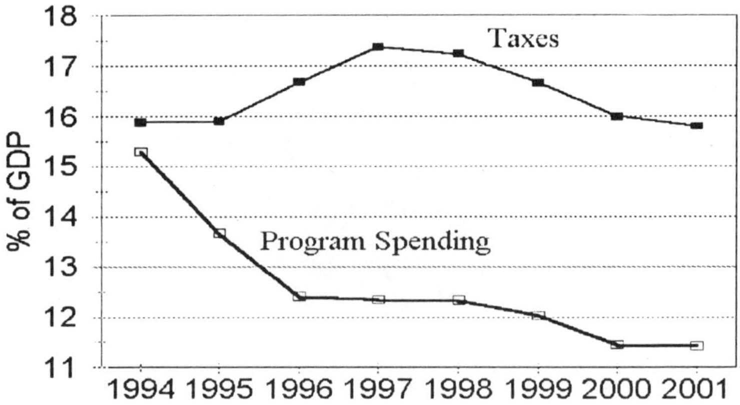

major tax cuts. Program spending for 1999 will equal just 12% of GDP — and that even includes the phony last-minute $2.5 billion allocation to future CHST transfers, money that will not be fully spent for years to come. It will dip even lower in the two years covered by this budget.

Program spending as a share of GDP may seem like an abstract concept, but the concrete social and economic manifestations of that sharp decline are painfully real: hospitals in crisis, soaring tuition fees, an underpaid and demoralized federal civil service, a crumbling public infrastructure at all levels, a continuing fiscal crisis in the Atlantic provinces, growing income inequality, an unemployment insurance system that excludes most of the unemployed — and the list goes on. All Canadians were shocked by the water poisoning tragedy that occurred in Walkerton, Ontario during the spring of 2000, the sort of thing usually associated with Third World countries, not with an advanced, industrial democracy. Yet disasters such as this may be only the tip of the iceberg, with the larger long-run consequences of the decline in public infrastructure still lurking below the surface.

Perhaps most distressing is not the damage that has been done to existing public services, but rather the failure of the government to use its moment of fiscal opportunity to initiate new programs that could make an essential contribution to our future health and social cohesion: the provision of ever-more-costly prescription drugs under the public health insurance system, the development of sensible home-care programs that would ease the crisis in our hospitals, or the provision of concrete early child development services informed by the overwhelming scientific evidence that quality preschool education is essential to lifetime intelligence and emotional well-being. Future generations of Canadians may wonder why we failed as a society to address these obvious needs; whatever our excuse will be, we certainly will not be able to claim it was because of a lack of money.

The lasting legacy of Paul Martin's tenure as finance minister will thus be roughly as follows: the deficit was vanquished. Taxes will have been cut to levels significantly below when the government was elected. Program spending will languish at its lowest levels in 60 years. And Canadian society will have become a leaner, meaner, more market-dominated place than even the most ambitious right-winger could have hoped for a decade ago. If these Liberals are a pack of "tax-and-spend socialists", how I would hate to watch what might happen under a group of real conservatives.

Canada's Tax Headache

It is taken for granted in most public discussions that Canadians pay too much in taxes. But "too much" is a relative term. Too much compared to what?

The usual answer is that we pay too much compared to Americans. On a collective basis we certainly pay more than Americans (although the average-income Canadian pays less tax than the average-income American). But we also have medicare, public universities, more generous public pensions and a range of other things that Canadians have typically indicated they are quite willing to pay for. Try as they might, Canada's business leaders have not yet succeeded in convincing us all of the strange proposition that the United States of America is the prototype against which all social and economic variables must be measured.

Do we pay "too much" compared to a broader sample of other countries? Not especially. Taxes collected by all levels of government in Canada almost exactly equal the average level for the Organization for Economic Cooperation and Development countries (OECD) as a whole: 43.5% in 1997, compared to 43.2% for the OECD, according to the OECD's own data.

Do we pay "too much" compared to how much we used to pay? Even here the evidence does not justify the unprecedented air time that has been captured by the denizens of tax rage. The tax revolt worked up a real head of steam through the latter 1990s. But ironically, that was the same decade in which taxes increased *less* than in any previous decade of the postwar era. Indeed, by a variety of measures there was hardly any increase in taxes in the 1990s at all.

Longer run trends in taxes and program spending by all levels of government in Canada are illustrated in Figure 3. Taxes increased significantly as a share of GDP during every decade of the postwar era, *until* the 1990s. Since 1990, total taxes collected at all levels (including CPP premiums) have remained stable at slightly above 45% of GDP.

Figure 3: Total Government Taxes and Spending (1950-2000, % of GDP)

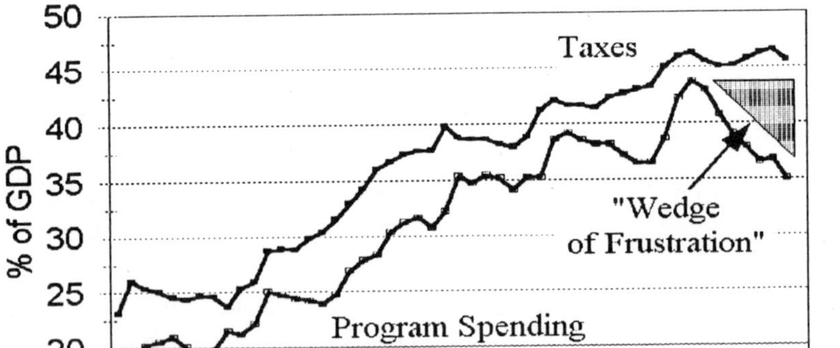

The role of higher taxes in the oft-discussed decline in real Canadian living standards during the 1990s has also been vastly overstated. Table 1 decomposes the decline in real per capita disposable incomes in Canada, a decline that reduced living standards by over 3% between 1990 and 1998, into its various components. Of the average income decline of $600 (in 1992 dollar terms), the vast majority, a full 98%, is accounted for by a decline in pre-tax "market" income. Yes, average personal taxes increased during the decade: by just over $400 per Canadian. But that increase was almost perfectly offset by an increase in personal transfer income (including public pensions) received from governments. On a net basis, governments can be blamed directly for all of $12 (or 2%) of the decline in real disposable incomes during this period. If we are looking for a scapegoat for the miserable performance of personal incomes in Canada in the 1990s, we have to point the finger at something other than taxes.

Table 1: Wages, Taxes and Living Standards: 1990 to 1998

1990 Disposable income per Canadian	$17,398
1998 Disposable income per Canadian	$16,798
Change	-$600
Decline in "market" incomes	-$588
Increase in taxes	+$413
Increase in government transfers	+$401
Net decline due to government	-$12 (2%)
Net decline due to "free market"	-$588 (98%)

Source: Author's calculations from Statistics Canada, *Canadian Economic Observer*; all figures expressed in real (1992$) terms.

There is one sense, however, in which Canadians may genuinely pay "too much" taxes, and this may help to explain some of the political basis for the tax rage movement. Canadians in aggregate now pay far more in taxes than the cost of the real programs and services which they receive in return for those taxes. As indicated in Figure 3, total taxes remained steady in the 1990s as a share of GDP, but government programs (again at all levels) declined sharply: from a peak of almost 45% early in the decade to just 35% of GDP by 1999. The downturn in program spending has opened up a significant and politically unstable "wedge" between what Canadians pay to government and what they get from government — termed a "wedge of frustration" in Figure 3.

That difference between taxes and programs, of course, is accounted for by the large debt-service charges paid at all levels of government, which ate up 17 cents of every dollar in government revenue last year, or about 8% of GDP. Happily, these debt charges will diminish quite rapidly in coming years as Canada's debt burden (measured as a share of GDP) erodes in the face of balanced budgets and continuing economic growth.

In the meantime, however, many Canadians feel they are getting a raw deal from government in return for their hard-earned tax payments. Whereas in past decades they willingly paid higher taxes in order to finance a desired expansion of public services (as Canada's social welfare system was constructed in the 1960s and 1970s), now they are grumpy about paying even the same amount that they used to pay, because they know they are no longer getting full value for their hard-earned contributions to the state.

The diminishing importance of debt-service charges will allow for a temporary but happy period during which both taxes can be cut and program spending can be increased (making it all the more puzzling that the Liberals have emphasized the former almost exclusively). Ultimately, however, once the debt burden is stabilized at some much lower level, the formerly close relationship between taxes and program spending will be re-established.

At that point, if Canadians want a dollar of increased public service, they will have to pay for it — as they did in spades during earlier decades. Alternatively, if they want a dollar in tax cuts, they will have to pay for that, too — in the form of forgone services. The current free lunch, which the federal government and many provinces are parcelling out so overwhelmingly in tax cuts, can last only for a while.

Where Did Taxes Come From?

This longer term view of the relationship between taxes and program spending puts some perspective on current emotional debates about taxes in Canada. Taxes are sometimes portrayed as some kind of mythical burden — a gigantic boulder which just tragically appeared on Canadians' shoulders one day, and which we have struggled to carry ever since. More sophisticated portrayals rely on various political-economy models in which narrowly self-interested politicians manipulate the system to raise revenues and spend them on pet projects.

Neither of these views is convincing. We pay taxes at the level we do today primarily because Canadians in past decades elected governments with mandates to collect those taxes and spend them. There are public services that Canadians want to consume, which constitute an important and valuable component of their overall consumption bundle, and which they are willing to pay for.

And there is no reason to expect that this sentiment will suddenly disappear. Polls clearly indicate that Canadians place a high value on most of the public services that they consume. International and historical data suggest, if anything, that public consumption is a *luxury* good, in the sense that people want *more* public services as their income levels rise (once they have covered the costs of private consumption essentials like food, clothing and shelter). Demographic and technological changes — such as those currently exerting such powerful effects on the economics of health care — also suggest that public service consumption is more likely to increase over time, not fall.

All of this is denied in the long-run planning documents of the federal government and most private sector analysts. These forecasts invariably project a continuing decline in program spending as a share of GDP in coming decades. The view underpinning these results is that Canadians are not interested in anything other than a minimal safety net of bare-bones social protections. Even if the Liberals actually followed their own 50:50 rule, federal program spending would likely just stabilize at its current low share of GDP. Other forecasts (which typically allow for only enough new spending to maintain existing public programs in constant real per capita terms) suggest continuing decline in the relative importance of public spending.

Forecasts like these may whet the appetite of conservatives looking for the maximum tax cut possible; if you freeze real per capita public spending at current levels, then the combination of economic growth and a shrinking debt burden would allow for tax cuts in coming years which would make Paul Martin's $58 billion seem, well, piddly by comparison. But all of these brave-new-world forecasts rest on the assumption that Canadians will tolerate a more or less permanent erosion in the relative importance of public consumption in their overall consumption bundles. On what theory of consumer choice do these analysts base their claim that Canadians, if presented with $100 in new income, would choose to spend exactly none of it on public services?

It is for all of these reasons that I hereby announce a most fearless millennium prediction. The "tax rage" which seems to wield such influence at present on the Canadian political landscape will be at most a passing fad. Most Canadians indicate they want more spending on health care, education and other programs, not less. The time will soon come when that new spending will require new taxes to fund it. And Canadians — surprise, surprise — will do so willingly. Indeed, by allocating so much of the current but temporary "free lunch" to tax cuts rather than to public programs, governments are simply ensuring that the tax cuts of today will be replaced by tax *increases* not so far down the road.

Taxes, Public Programs, and Inequality

Taxes, and the government programs that are financed from tax revenues, play a powerful role in reducing the degree of inequality in society, and enhancing the living standards of most Canadians. This is proven dramatically by recent data on income distribution.

Considering only the incomes that Canadians receive from the so-called "free market" (including wages, salaries, investment income and other forms of private income), inequality has widened significantly in the past decade. In 1989, the richest fifth of households in Canada earned 18 times as much from the "market" as the poorest fifth. By 1997, that ratio had reached 24-to-1 (see Figure 4).

Inequality is eased considerably, however, by government programs. In terms of disposable money income, the combination of income taxes (which are borne most heavily by high-income earners) and transfer payments such as Unemployment Insurance benefits or public pensions (received disproportionately by poorer Canadians) reduces this ratio of inequality by about two-thirds. After taxes and transfers, the richest fifth enjoys 7.6 times as much disposable income as the poorest, and this measure of inequality has *not* grown so much in the 1990s. The redistributive power of the tax-and-transfer system has thus largely offset — so far, anyway — the growing inequality of the private sector.

Figure 4: Inequality in Canada
(Before and after Government, 1997)

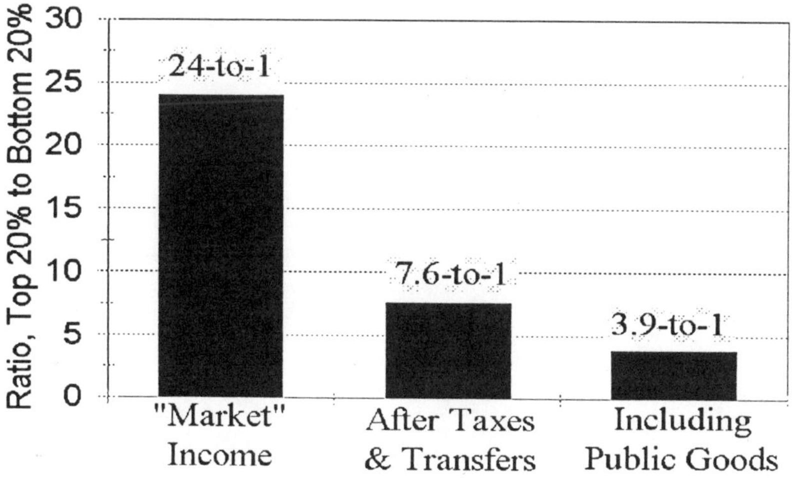

But the impact of public programs does not stop there. Non-cash public services (like health care, education, libraries, recreation facilities, etc.) form an important part of the total standard of living of most Canadians. These are forms of consumption that Canadians do not directly "buy", but which improve their standard of living nonetheless. For Canadians of modest means, this public consumption is very important. In 1997, each Canadian received on average some $13,200 worth of public services. (This assumes simply that each Canadian consumes an equal portion of the total public consumption bundle.) This is more than the total average household disposable income of the poorest fifth of society; hence, the living standard of poor people is essentially doubled by these non-cash public programs.

Even for middle-class Canadians, public programs account for 25% or more of total consumption. Once the value of public consumption is taken into account, then the ratio of total "income" of the top fifth falls to only 3.9 times as much as the poorest fifth.

By cutting taxes, and the programs they pay for, the federal government is ensuring that Canada will ultimately look more and more like the lopsided 24-to-1 society that is already typical of the purely private economy. It was one thing for purported Liberals to attack the deficit in as one-sided and painful manner as they did; principles are often set aside in times of crisis. But with its 2000 budget, this government has indicated that this is how it actually *wants* Canadian society to evolve. This has got to come as a shocking revelation to the millions of citizens who thought they were voting for a kinder, gentler Canada.

FISCAL STABILIZATION AND THE ALLOCATION OF FISCAL DIVIDEND: An Assessment

Pierre Fortin, Université du Québec à Montréal and Canadian Institute for Advanced Research

My assessment of the February 2000 federal budget will pertain mainly to the two old Musgrave (1959) categories of stabilization and allocation. I will append a few remarks on efficiency and fairness.

The End of Fiscal Stabilization

To begin with, let me emphasize that Canada's flexible exchange rate regime *cum* inflation targeting is inconsistent with any notion of fiscal stabilization policy. Broadly speaking, in the current policy framework the Bank of Canada sets the monetary conditions index (the MCI) to achieve some intermediate target level of real economic activity and, from there, the ultimate inflation target.[1] In setting the MCI at the desired level, the central bank takes into account to the fullest extent the demand-side factors other than the MCI that simultaneously affect output, *including fiscal policy*.

---

[1]The MCI is a linear combination of the real short-term interest rate controlled by the central bank and the market-determined real exchange rate.

The fact that fiscal policy suddenly becomes more expansionary would by itself tend to lift output above the target level and threaten to raise inflation above the target rate. However, being aware of this development, the monetary authority will react by increasing the MCI in order to prevent the undesired chain of events from taking place. In the end, real activity will be unchanged. In other words, under inflation targeting fiscal stabilization policy is meaningless.[2] Instead, through the central bank reaction function fiscal policy is better conceived of as affecting the real interest rate and the real exchange rate and, therefore, the *composition* of demand and output. It has consequences for allocation, not for stabilization. Expansionary policy leads to higher real interest rates and a real exchange rate appreciation. It therefore reduces investment and net exports as percentages of the gross domestic product (GDP): there is full crowding out. Restrictive fiscal policy has the opposite effect: there is full crowding in.

This kind of result is borne out by the simulations in the paper by Wilson, Dungan and Murphy (2001). They show that the impact of the February budget on output, which is already small at the unchanged level of the MCI, is reduced to almost nothing once the central bank reaction is taken into account.

The Allocation of Fiscal Dividend

The exit of stabilization brings the allocation function of fiscal policy to the forefront. Since its operating balance (excess of tax revenue over program spending) has become larger than its debt service, the federal government has

---

[2]In making this point, I omit one fine detail. Depending on the market reaction to policy developments, the exchange rate could appreciate and add some transitory negative pressure on inflation over and above the output effect. So, the central bank could allow output to increase during some adjustment period. But such dynamics are unlikely to change the final outcome. Basically, my description assumes that, on first approximation, the *common funnel theorem* holds: monetary and fiscal policy affect inflation only through their impact on aggregate demand and output.

entered the era of positive overall budgetary balance (or budget surplus). Thus, the new budget environment satisfies:

$$\text{Surplus} = \text{Tax revenue} - \text{Program spending} - \text{Debt service} \geq 0 .$$

From a macro perspective, the government must decide each year what to do with the underlying surplus (called the *fiscal dividend*) generated automatically by growing tax revenue (with unchanged tax parameters) and program spending (with, say, unchanged real per capita spending). Since debt service is exogenously determined by financial obligations inherited from past debt and interest rates, the allocation of fiscal dividend is by definition limited to three purposes: tax cuts, increases in program spending and debt reduction based on the residual surplus.

Budget planning starts with a projection of annual fiscal dividends over some planning horizon. This is exactly what the *Economic and Financial Update* of November 1999 presented in a very informative summary table (Canada. Department of Finance, 1999). An updated *fiscal dividend matrix* can be constructed with the help of this November document and various tables presented in the February *Budget Plan*. The outcome is layed out in Table 1.

The annual fiscal dividend is estimated to rise from 9.2 billion in 1999-2000 to 36.9 billion in 2004-05. The government's current two-year planning horizon ends in 2001-02. Beyond that, the potential for debt reduction exceeds the standard prudence factors, which indicates that future budgets could shift more of the dividend towards tax cuts or program spending, or else become more active in debt reduction. Tax cuts are delivered through moderate instalments averaging $3 billion per year from 2000-01 to 2003-04, and end with a large $9-billion initiative in 2004-05. Program spending remains under control. Following the 1999-2000 end-of-year increase of nearly $6 billion in program spending, later planned increases in spending over and above the constant real-per-capita baseline become more modest. The growth rate of nominal program spending is to average 2.9% annually between 1998-99 and 2002-03.

I review the budget strategy from the broad perspective of growth, efficiency and fairness, beginning with debt reduction, and then on with tax cuts and spending increases.

Table 1: The Fiscal Dividend Matrix: Budget Allocation of the Fiscal Dividend over Fiscal Years 1999-2000 to 2004-05 (Billions of dollars)

Year	*Tax Cuts*	*Increases in Program Spending*	*Potential for Debt Reduction*	*Total Dividend*
1999-2000	0.3	5.9	3.0	9.2
2000-01	4.6	3.1	4.0	11.7
2001-02	8.1	3.9	5.0	17.0
2002-03	10.6	4.0	8.8	23.4
2003-04	13.0	4.1	13.0	30.1
2004-05	22.1	4.2	10.6	36.9
Total	**58.7**	**25.2**	**44.4**	**128.3**

Note: The fiscal dividend for 1999-2000 incorporates only new tax and spending initiatives announced since the February 1999 budget. Tax measures are copied from chapters 1 and 4 of the *Budget Plan*. Program spending initiatives for the first four years are from chapter 1 of the *Plan*; for the last two years, they are projected by the author based on unchanged spending parameters. The "potential for debt reduction" for the first three years, also taken from chapter 1 of the *Plan*, is what remains of the fiscal dividend after subtracting tax cuts and spending increases. The budget makes sure this residual surplus matches the total amount set aside for economic prudence and as contingency reserve. Actual debt reduction will be equal to potential, less any use of these set-asides. The total fiscal dividend for the first three years is the sum of the three preceding items. To estimate the total fiscal dividend for the last three years, tax revenue is projected forward by annual increments of 5% from the pre-initiative level for 2001-02 ($176.1 billion), and pre-initiative estimates for program spending and debt service are taken directly from the November 1999 *Update*. The resulting balance gives the numbers reported in the last column. The potential for deficit reduction for the last three years is then calculated as residual by subtracting the already-estimated tax cuts and spending increases from the projected total fiscal dividend. All numbers are subject to revisions in future updates and budgets.

Source: Canada. Department of Finance (1999, 2000) and author's calculations.

The Debt-Reduction Strategy

The government's current debt strategy is clearly spelled out in the budget. For the new fiscal year, the targeted fiscal balance is a $3 billion surplus. This amount serves as contingency reserve against bad unforeseen events, so that the worst-case scenario is in fact an overall balance no lower than zero. In other words, for the new year the fiscal plan aims for nominal debt reduction of $3 billion at best and zero at worse. For later years, an economic prudence factor increasing with the length of the horizon is added to the contingency reserve.

The economic relevance of the debt strategy is that the debt-to-GDP ratio is going to be steadily reduced. Given that the numerator of this ratio, the nominal debt, is scheduled to remain unchanged or to decline slightly, a steady decline in the debt ratio will be automatically generated by increases in its denominator, nominal GDP. The debt burden is reduced not by absolute declines in the debt, but by the expanding size of the economy that sustains it. The rate of decrease of the debt-to-GDP ratio will fluctuate from year to year, but it can conservatively be expected to fall by two to three percentage points per year over the next decade, going down to 35% in 2010 from 60% in 2000.

Is this enough? Received economic theory expresses a firm judgement on the optimal amount of public debt as a percentage of GDP: "Set it so as to equate the marginal productivity of capital net of population growth to the social rate of time preference!" This is a great principle, but it is not easy to apply in practice. We simply do not know with much precision what the marginal productivity of capital is in the Canadian economy, or what the social rate of time preference of Canadians is (over and above what the notion really means).

Nevertheless, there is a strong presumption from existing empirical studies that the marginal productivity of capital is in excess of 10% per year, and that the social rate of time preference may be as low as 2% per year, especially if the welfare of future generations is taken into account. Since the difference, 8% per year, is much higher than the rate of population growth, the implication is that accumulated capital is much less than optimal in

Canada. A lower public debt-to-GDP ratio would encourage capital expansion by releasing a greater fraction of national saving for the financing of domestic private investment. In an open economy such as ours, part of the increase in welfare would come from the larger domestic capital stock induced by lower domestic interest rates, and part would arise from increased Canadian ownership of the capital stock installed both on Canadian territory and in other countries (i.e., our net external debt would fall).

Seen in this light, the optimal level of federal debt is likely to be zero, or even *negative*. (Negative debt means the federal government should be a net lender to the rest of the economy.) A straight back-of-envelope calculation would indicate that an increase of $600 billion (the approximate size of the current federal debt) in the capital stock of the Canadian economy from the current $2,000 billion or so would increase national income permanently by 8% and reduce the aggregate marginal productivity of capital by less than two percentage points.[3] This would still leave aggregate marginal productivity safely above the sum of the population growth rate and the social rate of time preference.

The policy implication of this argument is that the government's debt-reduction plan is in the right direction, but does not go far enough. We should not be satisfied until the federal debt has at least been eliminated. In addition to furthering economic growth and intergenerational equity, this would have three more advantages. First, the fiscal balance would become less sensitive to interest rate changes, which would ease budget planning considerably. Second, less taxes would eventually be needed to finance the debt service, which would help enhance economic efficiency. Third,

---

[3]If r is the marginal productivity of capital in the aggregate and α is the elasticity of aggregate real output (say y) with respect to capital (say k), then under standard assumptions about technology and competition the relationships $\Delta[\log(y)] = \alpha\Delta[\log(k)]$ and $\Delta r = [(\alpha - 1)r]\Delta[\log(k)]$ hold. Setting $\alpha = 0.3$, $r = 0.1$ and $\Delta[\log(k)] = \log(2600/2000)$ for illustrative purposes yields $\Delta[\log(y)] = 0.079$ and $\Delta r = -0.018$. This a closed-economy result, but the national income and welfare implications can be generalized to an open economy. There are some who argue that public debt reduction does not raise national income and output because any increase in public saving would be offset by an equal decrease in private saving — the so-called Ricardian equivalence proposition. But in the light of existing evidence, this empirical proposition remains without convincing support.

Canada's sovereignty would be strengthened through greater independence from the diktats of international lenders.

There is a (rather extreme) strategy under which the federal debt could be eliminated by 2010. The trick is to affect all annual fiscal dividends from 2000-01 on to pay off the debt. The required assumptions are that GDP and tax revenue increase by 5% annually, program spending rises by 3%, and the interest rate on the debt averages 7.2%. Once the debt is entirely eliminated in 2010, the accumulated $120 billion annual operating balance becomes available as (huge) fiscal dividend for tax cuts and program spending increases. From the very fact that by 2010 the debt service is brought down to zero, the tax burden can at that point be lowered *below* whatever level would have been otherwise achieved with less than full debt elimination. There is an intertemporal social choice to make. The choice is not between tax cuts and no tax cuts, but between small tax cuts now and large tax cuts later.

How realistic is this scenario? Not very much, in my view. The current political pressure for *immediate* tax cuts and program spending increases is strong, and a key election platform of the main opposition party, the Canadian Alliance, is to cut personal taxes by a very large amount. It will be difficult for the government to accelerate the process of debt reduction even by modest amounts. Let us at least thank God that the current zero-deficit policy, which has the debt-to-GDP ratio decline in sympathy with nominal GDP growth, seems to enjoy solid popular support.

The Tax Cuts

The budget plan calls for tax cuts reaching $22.1 billion in 2004-05, including 14.7 billion in personal taxes. How good is this in absolute terms, and relative to the $35 billion cut, including $30 billion in personal taxes, proposed by the Canadian Alliance Party? I think the budget plan fares well from both perspectives.

Above, I have expressed my view that the debt-reduction strategy is too timid. But taking now the latter as constraint, the relevant question is how to split the remainder of the fiscal dividend between tax cuts and increases in program spending. Judging the size of tax cuts is the same as judging the size of spending increases. Clearly, the end-of-fiscal-year $5.9 billion spurt in program expenditures for 1999-2000 has all the appearances of a spending binge. But over the four years 1999 to 2002, the planned average annual growth rate of nominal program spending looks quite reasonable: 2.9%, which is three percentage points less than the average growth rate of nominal GDP expected for the period by most forecasters. The budget's spending strategy therefore calls for a continuing decline in the program spending-to-GDP ratio, to about 11% in 2002-03 from 12.4% in 1998-99. Admittedly, future budgets may accelerate program spending. But we are at least off to a prudent start.

The Canadian Alliance Party has recently proposed to cut federal taxes by $35 billion instead of $22 billion (and personal taxes by $29 billion instead of $15 billion) by 2004-05. The Alliance's proposal raises three problems. First, it fails to offer a solution to the debt problem. From this perspective, it is just as bad as the government's plan.

Second, under any reasonable scenario for real growth and inflation, the Alliance's tax plan would require nominal program spending to increase by no more than 1.5% annually.[4] This means real spending per capita would fall in absolute terms until 2004-05. Not only would program spending restraint have to be very severe, but cuts in federal transfers to the provinces would likely generate intergovernmental conflicts, and the enormous pressure on health and education spending would have to be absorbed by provincial tax *increases*, with important consequences for the equilibrium of power in the

---

[4]From Table 1, a $35-billion tax cut by 2004-05 and a $7-billion prudence factor can be consistent with a $36.9-billion fiscal dividend only if program spending declines to $5.1 billion below its baseline projection, which the November 1999 *Update* set at $127.5 billion. This means program spending would have to increase from the currently-planned level of $116 billion in 2000-01 to $122.4 billion in 2004-05, implying an average annual growth rate of 1.4%. The popular counterpoint, that the tax cut itself will generate so much additional growth that it would pay for itself, is simply not acceptable on the basis of available empirical evidence.

federation. The Alliance's tax cuts, in other words, may not constitute a net gain at all for taxpayers, and for supporters of intergovernmental peace.

Third, the Alliance's personal tax cut would feature a flat rate of 17% on taxable income and increased tax shelters for high-income earners. This would make it an extremely regressive tax initiative. Table 2 clarifies the picture by comparing the reductions in tax liabilities for three standard taxpayers earning $30,000, $50,000 and $100,000, respectively, brought about by the Liberal and Alliance personal tax plans in 2004-05. The Alliance tax cut is, on average, twice as large as the Liberal tax cut. It is also heavily tilted towards high-income earners; it is, in fact, very precisely targeted on them.

Table 2: Federal Income Tax Liability of "Standard" Taxpayer (No children)

Total Income of Taxpayer	*Year 1999 Tax*	*Liberals 2004*		*Alliance 2004*	
		Tax	*Reduction*	*Tax*	*Reduction*
$	$	$	%	$	%
30,000	2,977	2,745	-7.8	2,415	-18.9
50,000	6,991	6,006	-14.1	5,199	-25.6
100,000	19,739	17,001	-13.9	12,084	-38.8

Note: The "standard" taxpayer takes advantage of only three non-refundable tax credits: the basic personal exemption, the Canada Pension Plan contribution and the Employment Insurance premium. He or she also makes average use of RPP and RRSP deductions within the income class. About 75% of taxpayers have no children.

Source: Author's calculations from various official documents.

Efficiency and Fairness Issues

The budget has interesting implications for efficiency and fairness. On efficiency, there is a welcome bias of new spending initiatives towards growth-enhancing public investment (research and innovation, environmental technologies and infrastructures).

The general effect of tax cuts is also to increase economic efficiency — you need not be a Reagan supply-sider to believe taxation generates economic waste. I have three observations to offer in this respect. First, even if the empirical evidence on the effect of international tax differentials on migration is weak, it is a matter of elementary prudence to avoid excessively large personal tax differentials with the United States in the case of higher incomes. While the Alliance's tax proposal may go too far in that direction, the budget may be too timid.

Second, there is some effort in the budget to reduce the very high marginal tax rates (in excess of 60% if provincial taxes are included) around incomes slightly above $30,000. These were generated by the lack of indexing and the accumulation of refundable tax credits that have to be recovered as income rises. The increase to $35,000 of the level of income at which the middle tax bracket begins to apply, the reduction of the middle tax rate to 23% from 26%, and the full indexation of the personal tax all concur to this end.

Third, the budget is too hesitant to use personal and corporate taxation to encourage saving and investment directly. In contrast with the Alliance's proposal, personal ceilings on Registered Retirement Savings Plans (RRSPs) are not increased. The treatment of investment outlays in corporate taxation is not ameliorated. While the announced reduction of the corporate tax rate to 21% from 28% is welcome, it will still take five years to take effect fully. In 2004 the OECD median will already be much lower.

Finally, I have a major quibble with the way horizontal equity has been redefined in Ottawa over the past two decades. If my neighbour and I both have total incomes of $100,000, but he has five cats and no children while I have no cats and five children, we get exactly the same tax treatment. With respect, I do not believe this is fair. So I hail the Alliance's proposal to reintroduce a standard and universal deduction of $3,000 per child into the personal tax form. Further, I fail to see why essential needs would vary with income. It is hard to understand why and how the Department of Finance has come to determine that the opposite is true.

Conclusion

Let me summarize my views around three statements. First, forget about fiscal stabilization. Under the current flexible exchange rate regime with inflation targeting, the central bank reaction function will always offset any expansionary or restrictive effect of fiscal policy automatically. This makes fiscal stabilization obsolete even in the very short run.

Second, the February 2000 budget announces significant tax cuts, prudent spending growth, and very modest reductions in the nominal federal debt. Based on standard economic principles, a strong argument can be made that the entire federal debt should be retired without too much delay, and that future budgets should do (much) more in this area.

Third, with the current debt strategy as constraint, the announced tax cuts and spending growth path look reasonable. The alternative proposal by the Canadian Alliance Party calls for personal tax cuts twice as large as planned in the budget. Its suggested increase in personal ceilings on RRSPs would encourage personal savings, and its proposed flat deduction per child would restore some of the lost horizontal equity in the Canadian personal tax system. But the Alliance's platform is oblivious to the lingering debt problem, it would imply very severe continuing restraint in federal program spending, and it has an extremely regressive bias.

References

Canada. Department of Finance (1999), *Economic and Fiscal Update* (Ottawa: Department of Finance).

_________ (2000), *The Budget Plan* (Ottawa: Department of Finance).

Musgrave, R.A. (1959), *The Theory of Public Finance* (New York: McGraw-Hill).

Wilson, T.A., P. Dungan and S. Murphy (2001), "Macroeconomic Effects of Budget 2000", in this volume.

Session Seven
BUDGETING IN THE NEW MILLENNIUM

SOME REFLECTIONS ON THE BUDGET PROCESS AND THE FISCAL ISSUES CONFRONTING CANADA

Jack M. Mintz

The proceedings of this conference provide much good analysis and debate of the most important issues addressed by the 2000 budget. Instead of trying to summarize the highlights of the discussions, I thought I would provide an overall assessment of the budget process and the fiscal issues confronting Canada. This would tie in nicely with the many points raised by the participants in the conference.

I also benefit from writing this summary after the presentation of the mini-budget in October 2000. Some of the proposed changes in the October mini-budget will be briefly mentioned below.

The Budget Process

The current budget process has been significantly improved with the 2000 budget, although there is still some way to go to make clear what fiscal objectives are to be pursued by the federal government. Let me expand on this point by going back to 1993 when the current government began its reign.

At the inception of its power, the Liberals were facing a major crisis brought on by over a decade and a half of fiscal mismanagement. Total government debt, as a proportion of gross domestic product (GDP), was well over 100%. Foreign indebtedness was quite high by OECD standards: over 40% of GDP. The annual federal deficit was almost $45 billion, the highest level ever after a ten-year string of deficits that rarely got below $30 billion annually. After a year in power, the minister of finance, Paul Martin, made the elimination of the deficit the fiscal objective for the federal government. Each year, a proposed target deficit for two years was chosen using forecasts that were pessimistic compared to the average private-sector forecasts for the economy. Even a contingency reserve of $3 billion was established: the amount would not be spent but reserved for the retirement of debt. The minister was highly successful with this approach. He not only achieved but also overshot his target, therefore creating much needed fiscal credibility for the Department of Finance. The government as a whole along with the public understood Canada's main fiscal objective — deficit elimination — thereby making it more possible to cut expenditures.

With the deficit eliminated by 1997, the federal government lost its fiscal objective. The Liberals in the 1997 election proposed to follow a policy that upcoming fiscal surpluses would be split 50/50 between expenditure on the one hand and tax and debt relief on the other. The department continued following its procedure of prudently forecasting surpluses over a two-year cycle and a $3 billion contingency reserve to retire market debt. However, fiscal surpluses would grow well beyond the predicted amounts within the year. Moreover, the 50/50 rule could be easily manipulated (for example, a targeted tax cut can be treated either as a tax cut or an expenditure). Thus, the government began to lose fiscal credibility for two reasons. First, the public no longer understood the fiscal objective for the economy once the deficit was eliminated. Second, a bias grew to devote unforecasted surpluses to one-time expenditure increases (front-loaded by creating a fund like the Canada Foundation for Innovation in which the money would be spent over several years). On the other hand, it would be difficult to cut taxes on a permanent scale from one-time unanticipated surpluses.[1]

---

[1]For these reasons, Mintz and Poschmann (1999) called for a multi-year plan to be adopted for tax cuts so that more of the surplus would be devoted to tax relief.

The 2000 budget for the first time introduces two important innovations. The first is to provide a five-year plan for tax cuts. The minister was still reluctant to commit to a specific path of changes beyond the first two years, but total tax cuts were indicated to take place within five years.[2] Thus, a five-year period was clearly longer than fiscal periods used for projections. The second was to include a "prudence factor" that shows the degree to which the forecasted surplus was expected to be pessimistic relative to average private-sector forecast. This factor gives rise to an additional surplus that could arguably be used for further debt reduction.

What is Needed to Improve the Budget Process

While the move to the five-year plan was a milestone, there remain several problems to the current budgetary approach. These are related to a lack of clarity and transparency since the surplus is undefined, incremental decision making, pro-cyclical rather than anti-cyclical fiscal policy and a lack of a clear fiscal objective for planning.

- *Lack of clarity and transparency*. The fiscal surplus is a somewhat nebulous concept to define. It can be calculated by computing surpluses, based on expenditures assumed to grow with only prices, prices plus population, GDP or some other variant. The minister engaged a group of private-sector forecasters to provide estimates of the surplus according to the assumption that expenditures would grow with population and prices. This might be a sensible approach, but it by no means suggests that there is an overall consensus as to how much government should grow in the future. The size of government is an issue discussed by various authors in this publication.

---

[2]Subsequent to the 2000 budget, the federal government devoted a much larger amount of surplus to debt reduction for the fiscal year 1999-2000. Further, the October mini-budget sped up the tax reductions, committed to these reductions over a period longer than two years, increased some and projected a greater amount of surplus to debt reduction.

- *Incremental fiscal decisions*. The fiscal surplus is believed to be some magical pot that is divided among competing purposes. The focus on the surplus, far too excessive in my view, provides an impression of a zero-sum game — anyone in favour of tax cuts, for example, is against expenditures on health care and education. Worst of all, planning on the basis of surpluses encourages incremental decision making in that expenditure priorities and tax cuts are only to be funded by the excess of revenues over to some baseline concept of expenditures. By implication, there is no room for reallocating expenditures by cutting some expenditure programs to make room to fund new priorities. Nor are tax cuts being partly financed by broadening the tax base. In other words, there is no plan to reform expenditure programs or taxes, only just spend more money in certain priority areas.

- *Pro-cyclical fiscal policy*. The current approach to fiscal planning has the potential to destabilize the economy. Rather than taking the view of running large surpluses during good times with potential deficits during bad times, the current budgetary process would do the opposite. Expenditures are ramped up or taxes are cut to keep surpluses small during expansions and expenditures are cut and taxes are increased to avoid deficits during recessions. Perhaps, it is viewed that fiscal policy can no longer stabilize the economy. However, certainly fiscal policy no longer provides the government a tool that could complement monetary policy, for example, interest rates would need to be raised to combat inflationary pressures rather than dampening the economy with more strict fiscal discipline.

- *Lack of fiscal objective*. The current rule that 50% of surpluses are to be expended on new programs with the remainder devoted to tax cuts and debt relief does not provide a clear economic plan for the economy. Is 50% of surplus too much or too little in terms of funding federal programs? How much of tax revenues are needed by the government to fund its priorities? How quickly does the debt/GDP ratio (now about 85%) need to be reduced. There is thus a fuzzy commitment to spend, cut taxes and reduce debt without any clear goals. Perhaps a new fiscal objective is needed. For example, if the fiscal objective is a total government debt/GDP ratio of about 25% by 2015,[3] the federal and provincial governments should be running surpluses close to $25 billion now. As Fortin (2001) mentions in his paper, reducing debt is a clear priority. If so, why not establish a clear target? An alternative fiscal objective would be to establish a target ratio of government expenditure to GDP. This could provide an indication as to how large governments need to be in the economy. Canadians can then debate the role of government in establishing such a target.

Elements of an Economic Plan

The main point to the above comments is that there is a need to incorporate economic planning as part of the fiscal plan of governments. This requires a continuous review of the effectiveness of public expenditures, the structure of taxes and the overall plan for fiscal health. A fiscal target is critical for planning purposes so that both government departments and the public understand the constraints faced by governments in raising taxes and debt to finance public expenditures. Below, I would like to suggest which elements of an economic plan should be considered for better fiscal planning.

Identifying the Objectives

The first step is to identify the challenges faced by the economy and to establish priorities in order to identify the fiscal tools needed to achieve objectives. Whether it is meeting the needs of the new economy, improving opportunities for employment in a global economy, or dealing with the demographic challenges of the future, it is important for governments to make clear what should be the primary thrusts of policy. The challenges of the new economy, for example, suggest increased attention should be paid to investment, savings and education. Jobs mean concentrating on employment

---

[3]New Zealand has a target debt/GDP ratio in the range of 20% to 30% (which it has now accomplished).

prospects for the economy in an increasingly competitive economy. Demographic challenges put more emphasis on the potential debt liabilities left for the working generation of tomorrow.

Debt

Although federal and provincial governments should be commended for the significant steps made to eliminating deficits and reducing debt, there remains an excessively high debt burden: almost 85% of GDP. The debt burden is an issue that should be of significant concern, given Canada's demographics. The debt burden, as we measure it, does not include other forms of unfunded liabilities which face future working populations, including publicly provided health-care programs. With the aging of the population and low fertility rates, the number of working-age Canadians will actually begin declining in numbers by the year 2020. Given the importance of programs that provide substantial income or in-kind support for the elderly, including old age security and health care, taxes on the working population can rise substantially over the next two decades to fund elderly benefits. This declining working population base is an issue being faced by virtually all industrialized nations so that keen competition for labour at the international level will appear, creating substantial pressures on any country facing rising tax rates in order to fund benefits. Thus, it is important that Canada continually address the debt problem by reducing the debt burden.

The current situation in which a significant portion of unanticipated surpluses is spent on new programs rather than drawing down the debt is most disappointing in this regard. To simply expect to run surpluses of only $3 billion at the federal level with some smaller amounts (except Alberta) at the provincial level is, in my view, quite unacceptable. Governments were not shy in running deficits that were well in excess of $40 billion in the 1980s. Why not run larger surpluses?

As mentioned above, if all governments in Canada ran an annual surplus of $25 billion per year for the next 15 years, we could reduce the debt/GDP ratio to about 25% by 2015. This would provide significant savings in public debt charges to accommodate the expenditures needed on health care and other programs needed by a modern day economy with an aging population and declining workforce. A debt/GDP ratio target helps the public understand why large surpluses are necessary.

It is pleasing to note that the federal government did run a much larger surplus for 1999-2000 that will make a greater contribution to debt reduction. However, there remains no clear commitment to running larger surpluses in order to reduce the debt burden much faster in the future.

Expenditures

A missing element is a review of expenditure priorities within the budget process. While there is a clear process to set priorities for new spending (paid from growing surpluses), there is no attempt at the federal level to look at *existing* programs in order to reallocate funds from unnecessary programs for priorities. The House of Commons' finance committee did recommend that each department should evaluate its expenditure programs by using a set of criteria that would determine their effectiveness. However, this recommendation has not been seriously considered.

There are good reasons to undertake expenditure reviews on a continuing basis. Economic studies, such as Kneller, Bleaney and Gemmell (1999), suggest that productive government expenditures, including health, education and infrastructure, increase per capita growth rates in the economy while distortionary taxes, such as taxes on capital and high personal income taxes, will lower them. Thus, to the extent that taxes are used to finance productive expenditures, the impact is potentially to increase or, at least, to not impair growth in per capita incomes. On the other hand, distortionary taxes used to finance non-productive public expenditures can impact negatively on growth. Thus, it is important for governments to make sure that tax revenues are used to fund those programs that are effective, otherwise the economic cost of taxation is excessively high. Therefore, it does not seem inappropriate to make sure that our expenditure programs are effective.

Tax Cuts or Tax Reform

The current process of cutting taxes is disappointing in that governments are giving up a golden opportunity to reform the tax system in order to make it more efficient and fair while lowering tax burdens. While the cuts to personal income and corporate income tax rates are arguably important, there should be an attempt to eliminate ineffective incentives. The 2000 budget does make some headway in trying to deal with some of the incentives in the system, such as those related to the tax treatment of inbound investment and resource write-offs, but the budget fails to broaden its approach at looking at incentives at a more general level. Several speakers suggested that tax reform is needed, especially with respect to the treatment of capital income taxation. Perhaps, greater effort will be needed to move to a consumption tax in order to encourage savings and growth.

Another important issue is the relation of income transfer programs with the personal income tax. Canada has gone a long way in reducing administrative costs of transfer programs by providing refundable tax credits for the poor (including the child tax benefit and GST credit), in addition to grants that are clawed back, such as the old age guaranteed income supplement. The income-tested supplements result in higher marginal tax rates, especially for lower income tax brackets. One view expressed at the conference is the need to reduce such claw-back rates while some argued that it is optimal to impose taxes and social policy in this manner. I accept the latter view that it is not inappropriate to have higher effective marginal tax rates at lower levels of income compared to those rates at middle and upper income levels in order to accomplish both efficiency and equity objectives. My concern, however, is the overall rates. It seems that effective federal-provincial tax rates in excess of 80% (such as around $30,000 in individual income) seem far too high, potentially discouraging work effort and savings. Personal income tax rates may be too high in general as some authors did point out.

Federal-Provincial Issues

No policy issue in Canada can be discussed without recognizing the importance of both federal and provincial governments in formulating policy. Transfers for health care are being ramped up (including the agreement that followed the February 2000 budget in September). There may be some evidence of increased reliance on conditional transfers such as for infrastructure, medical equipment and postsecondary education. All these issues raise important questions related to fiscal federalism. For example, does the public understand which level of government is accountable for Canada's health-care system? Is there too much game-playing whereby governments seek both to blame others for the mistakes and to take credit for the positive outcomes? Are we necessarily getting the right political economy whereby the government responsible for decision making must raise the funds to pay for their decisions?

These kinds of issues are going to be of increasing importance in the next two years. Few noted the greater degree of tax competition among the provinces, including recent initiatives to lower business tax rates in Alberta and Ontario. The poorer provinces will face increased pressure to match these moves. At the same time, many of the provinces have little room left to cut expenditures on health, education and infrastructure. Thus, there will be increased pressure for the federal government to give resources to the provinces.

What form of assistance should provinces expect? Will there be more intergovernmental grants or increased room to raise taxes with reductions at the federal level? Accountability will be better served if the federal government transfers tax points to the provinces to fund their own priorities. However, the poorer provinces, with less fiscal capacity, would require greater expenditure grants, such as equalization, if they are to support their current programs.

With a potential recession in the United States, the room for the federal government to provide funding for provinces will be more difficult unless it constrains its own program expenditures.

Conclusions

This conference presented a useful review of the 2000 budget. The important points raised by many of the participants should be revisited at the next conference of a similar topic. I am sure the debate will be as exciting and interesting as the discussion contained in this volume.

References

Fortin, P. (2001), "Fiscal Stabilization and the Allocation of Fiscal Dividend: An Assessment", this volume.

Kneller, R., M.F. Bleaney and N. Gemmell (1999), "Fiscal Policy and Growth: Evidence from the OECD Countries", *Journal of Public Economics* 74, 171-190.

Mintz, J. and F. Poschmann (1999), *Tax Reform, Tax Reduction: The Missing Framework*, C.D. Howe Institute Commentary No. 121 (Toronto: C.D. Howe Institute).

CONTRIBUTORS

Keith Banting	School of Policy Studies, Queen's University
Lise Bastarache	Royal Bank of Canada, Montreal
Robin Boadway	Department of Economics, Queen's University
Thomas J. Courchene	John Deutsch Institute, Queen's University
Peter Dungan	Institute for Policy Analysis, University of Toronto
Rick Egelton	Bank of Montreal, Toronto
Pierre Fortin	Département d'économique, Université du Québec à Montréal and Canadian Institute for Advanced Research
Harvey Lazar	Institute of Intergovernmental Relations, Queen's University
Jack Mintz	Rotman School of Management, University of Toronto and C.D. Howe Institute, Toronto
Steve Murphy	Institute for Policy Analysis, University of Toronto
Lars Osberg	Department of Economics, Dalhousie University
William B.P. Robson	C.D. Howe Institute, Toronto
Michael Smart	Department of Economics, University of Toronto
Gregor Smith	Department of Economics, Queen's University
Jim Stanford	Canadian Auto Workers, Toronto
Thomas A. Wilson	Institute for Policy Analysis, University of Toronto
Frances Woolley	Department of Economics, Carleton University

PUBLICATIONS OF THE JOHN DEUTSCH INSTITUTE

Policy Forum Series

F1. *Industrial Strategy*, Richard G. Harris, 1983.
F2. *The Federal Budget of 1983*, Neil Bruce, 1983.
F3. *Medicare in an Age of Restraint*, William G. Watson, 1984.
F4. *Special Import Measures Legislation*, Klaus Stegemann, 1985.
F5. *Tax Reform and the Consumption Tax*, Jack M. Mintz, 1985.
F6. *The International Debt Problem*, Gordon R. Sparks, 1985.
F7. *Reform of the Bankruptcy Act*, Frank Lewis, 1986.
F8. *Universality and Social Policies in the '80s*, Alan Green and Nancy Olewiler, 1985.
F9. *The May 1985 Federal Budget*, Douglas D. Purvis, 1985.
F10. *The February 1986 Federal Budget*, Martin F.J. Prachowny, 1986.
F11. *Reform of the Corporate Income Tax System*, Jack M. Mintz and Douglas D. Purvis, 1987.
F12. *Business Transfer Tax*, Robin W. Boadway and Jack M. Mintz, 1987.
F13. *Rent Controls in Ontario*, Richard J. Arnott and Jack M. Mintz, 1987.
F14. *Macropolicy Issues in the Medium Term*, Jack M. Mintz and Douglas D. Purvis, 1989.
F15. *The Role of Immigration in Canada's Future*, Charles M. Beach and Alan G. Green, 1988.
F16. *Public Sector Management*, R. Gordon Cassidy and Jack M. Mintz, 1989.
F17. *The February 1990 Federal Budget*, Martin F.J. Prachowny, 1990.
F18. *Canadian Transportation Policy*, David W. Gillen, 1990.
F19. *Takeovers and Tax Policy*, Jack M. Mintz, 1990.
F20. *Pay Equity: Means and Ends*, Michael G. Abbott, 1990.
F21. *Europe 1992 and the Implications for Canada*, Douglas D. Purvis, 1991.
F22. *Economic Developments in the Soviet Union and Eastern Europe: Implications for Canada*, Douglas D. Purvis, 1991.
F23. *The February 1991 Federal Budget*, Martin F.J. Prachowny and Douglas D. Purvis, 1991.
F24. *North American Free Trade Area*, William G. Watson, 1991.
F25. *Economic Aspects of the Federal Government's Constitutional Proposals*, Robin W. Boadway and Douglas D. Purvis, 1991.
F26. *The February 1992 Federal Budget*, Thomas J. Courchene and Martin F.J. Prachowny, 1992.
F27. *Tax Effects on the Financing of Medium and Small Public Corporations*, Roy D. Hogg and Jack M. Mintz, 1992.
F28. *Tax Policy for Turbulent Times*, Roy D. Hogg and Jack M. Mintz (eds.), 1993.
F29. *Deficits and Debt in the Canadian Economy*, Richard G. Harris (ed.), 1993.
F30. *Capital Budgeting in the Public Sector*, Jack M. Mintz and Ross S. Preston (eds.), 1993.
F31. *Financial Derivatives: Managing and Regulating Off-Balance Sheet Risks*, Thomas J. Courchene and Edwin H. Neave (eds.), 1994.
F32. *Who Pays the Piper?: Canada's Social Policy*, Roy D. Hogg and Jack M. Mintz (eds.), 1995.
F33. *The 1995 Federal Budget: Retrospect and Prospect*, Thomas J. Courchene and Thomas A. Wilson (eds.), 1995.
F34. *Reforming the Canadian Financial Sector: Canada in Global Perspective*, Thomas J. Courchene and Edwin H. Neave (eds.), 1997.
F35. *The 1997 Federal Budget: Retrospect and Prospect*, Thomas J. Courchene and Thomas A. Wilson (eds.), 1997.
F36. *Equalization: Its Contribution to Canada's Economic and Fiscal Progress*, Robin W. Boadway and Paul A.R. Hobson (eds.), 1998.
F37. *The 2000 Federal Budget: Retrospect and Prospect*, Paul A.R. Hobson and Thomas A. Wilson (eds.), 2001.

Roundtable Series

R1. *Canadian Balance of Payments, Perspectives and Policy Issues*, Douglas D. Purvis (ed.), 1983.
R2. *Economic Adjustment and Public Policy in Canada*, Douglas D. Purvis (ed.), 1984.
R3. *Declining Productivity and Growth*, Douglas D. Purvis (ed.), 1985.
R4. *The Impact of Taxation on Business Activity*, Jack M. Mintz and Douglas D. Purvis (eds.), 1987.
R5. *Rent Control: The International Experience*, Richard J. Arnott and Jack M. Mintz (eds.), 1987.
R6. *Economic Impacts of Tax Reform*, Jack M. Mintz and John Whalley (eds.), published by the Canadian Tax Foundation, 1989.
R7. *Tax Expenditures and Government Policy*, Neil Bruce (ed.), 1988 (French version also available).
R8. *Economic Dimensions of Constitutional Change*, Robin W. Boadway, Thomas J. Courchene and Douglas D. Purvis (eds.), 2 Volumes, 1991.
R9. *The Future of Fiscal Federalism*, Keith G. Banting, Douglas M. Brown and Thomas J. Courchene (eds.), published jointly with School of Policy Studies and Institute of Intergovernmental Relations, 1994.
R10. *Infrastructure and Competitiveness*, Jack M. Mintz and Ross S. Preston (eds.), 1994.
R11. *Transition and Structural Change in the North American Labour Market*, Michael G. Abbott, Charles M. Beach and Richard P. Chaykowski (eds.), 1997 (published jointly with and available from IRC Press, Industrial Relations Centre).
R12. *Fiscal Targets and Economic Growth*, Thomas J. Courchene and Thomas A. Wilson (eds.), 1998.

Bell Canada Papers Series

B1. *Productivity, Growth and Canada's International Competitiveness*, Thomas J. Courchene and Douglas D. Purvis (eds.), 1993.
B2. *Stabilization, Growth and Distribution: Linkages in the Knowledge Era*, Thomas J. Courchene (ed.), 1994.
B3. *Technology, Information and Public Policy*, Thomas J. Courchene (ed.), 1995.
B4. *Policy Frameworks for a Knowledge Economy*, Thomas J. Courchene (ed.), 1996.
B5. *The Nation State in a Global/Information Era: Policy Challenges*, Thomas J. Courchene (ed.), 1997.
B6. *Room to Manoeuvre? Globalization and Policy Convergence*, Thomas J. Courchene (ed.), 1999.

Walwyn Lecture Series

W1. *Regulatory Reform and the Search for Solvency*, Henry N.R. Jackman, 1987.
W2. *Capital Management vs Operations Management*, Marshall A. (Mickey) Cohen, 1987.
W3. *Free Trade: What's in it for You?* Hon. Gerald A. Regan, 1989.
W4. *Economic Growth in the Coming Years: What it Means for a Community*, Marcel Côté, 1992.

Monographs

Women and Work, Richard P. Chaykowski and Lisa M. Powell (eds.), 1999.